"*The More I Learn, The More I Love* is a beautifully written book that provides life-changing advice on self-discovery and personal development. Whether you need to break out of a negative pattern or simply create more balance in your life, this book will help pave the way. Wendy Ditta reveals the methods and principles for breaking through and achieving true and sustainable happiness and success. This book is a gold mind of guidance to turn your life around."

Peggy McColl
New York Times Best-Selling Author

"You won't put down *The More I Learn, The More I Love* until you've completed it. I made the mistake of thinking I could just read a few chapters before going to bed. But I was mistaken. I was hooked halfway through chapter one. This book is a must-read book and it will change the way you look at your life. It teaches you to see life through the lens of love, and while doing so you will discover a beautiful space of all the infinite possibilities that love will unveil right before your very eyes."

Dr. Jussi Eerikäinen
Cardiologist, Neuroplasticity Researcher & Best-Selling Author

"You will benefit from reading Wendy Ditta's *The More I Learn, The More I Love*. Her authenticity about transforming from "Gangsta to Goddess" radiates with each turn of the page. This book will touch your heart by inspiring a blend of self discovery and personal development. If you are ready to create a life by design, then this book will show you how to change the way you think so you can live your life on purpose."

M. Shawn Petersen
International Best-Selling Author of *Stella and the Timekeepers*

"I love this book! Wendy clearly articulates what is required to share your gifts with the world and break free of the false ideas that hold us back. Her perspective was a breath of fresh air that has forever altered the way I look at things."

Brian Proctor
Co-Author of *Darn Easy*
VP of Business Development for Proctor Gallagher Institute

"Wendy Ditta reminds us that there's always an opportunity for peace in every situation. *The More I Learn, The More I Love* is thought provoking and provides easy steps to create a life that gives you life! It's a must read for anyone wanting to tune more deeply into the desires of their heart!"

Cynthia Kersey
Best-Selling Author, *Unstoppable & Unstoppable Women*

"Success follows a great game plan. Wendy Ditta is a tremendous learner, and as a result she is a tremendous teacher with valuable insights. *The More I Learn, The More I Love* is a brilliant message for reconnecting to self through simple and actionable life-changing lessons. Read this book if you want to live with peace, purpose, and happiness and to make a positive difference in others for good. I can't think of anything more important than learning and living the message of this book."

Dr. Carla Ferrer Russo, PhD., ND., RYT
CEO, Zen Wellness Academy

"Wendy's refreshing vulnerability is endearing and inspiring. In fact, this was the very quality that brought about her pivotal shift from "Gangtsa to Goddess." Through this amazing blend of structure and stories you now have a roadmap to the life you deserve."

Jae M. Rang, Strategist, Author, Mom www.jaeassociates.com

"Wendy Ditta's book, *The More I Learn, The More I Love* reminds us of our core Selves and how to access our true Selves once again, despite the challenges and setbacks. Gratitude and allowance, wrapped in laughter and levity bring us back to our core Self. A must read and gift to your loved ones."

Banafsheh Akhlaghi, Esq. International Best-selling author of *Beautiful Reminders: Anew, attorney, and social entrepeneur*

"In *The More I Learn, The More I Love*, Wendy Ditta reminds us that Love is spiritual truth expressed as reality through our words and deeds. To love more, we need to grow more. This book will help you accomplish just that."

Lennox Cornwall, author of *Embracing Failure: Your Key to Success*

"Wendy has learned and is demonstrating one of the great secrets of life. Even if you only study one chapter in *The More I Learn, The More I Love*, you will benefit greatly."

Sandy Gallagher
CEO & Co-Founder
Proctor Gallagher Institute

"Happiness comes when we figure out how to acknowledge the things we can't change and are content with what we have. By reading this book, I learned to unlock the potential that was hidden inside me all along, to ask for what I wanted and embrace new opportunities. *The More I Learn, The More I Love* reveals the specific requirements, methods and principles for breaking through and achieving success in life, work, health and love."

Judy O'Beirn, Creator & Co-Author of the International Bestselling *Unwavering Strength* Series

Published by
Hasmark Publishing, judy@hasmarkservices.com

Copyright © 2018 Wendy Ditta
First Edition 2017

Disclaimer

This book is designed to provide information and motivation to our readers. It is sold with the understanding that the publisher is not engaged to render any type of psychological, legal, or any other kind of professional advice. The content of each article is the sole expression and opinion of its author, and not necessarily that of the publisher. No warranties or guarantees are expressed or implied by the publisher's choice to include any of the content in this volume. Neither the publisher nor the individual author(s) shall be liable for any physical, psychological, emotional, financial, or commercial damages, including, but not limited to, special, incidental, consequential or other damages. Our views and rights are the same: You are responsible for your own choices, actions, and results.

Permission should be addressed in writing to Wendy Ditta:
info@lifemasteryandbeyond.com

Cover Design, Patti Knoles
patti@virtualgraphicartsdepartment.com

Editor, Justin Spizman
justin@justinspizman.com

Book Layout, Anne Karklins
annekarklins@gmail.com

ISBN-13: 978-1-988071-52-7
ISBN-10: 1988071526

Hasmark
PUBLISHING

THE MORE I
LEARN

THE MORE I

WENDY DITTA

I lovingly dedicate this book to my husband, Keefe.
Thank you for encouraging me to stand in
my creative power. Your continued love and support has
fueled me with passion to proceed full speed ahead.
You have been a tremendous role model exuding courage,
strength, and persistence in all that you do.
Thank you for being by my side, co-creating our most
desired dreams and an everlasting love. I love you.
xoxo

ACKNOWLEDGEMENTS

Grateful acknowledgement is given to my brilliant friend and mentor, *New York Times* bestselling author Peggy McColl. Your loving nudges, expert advice, and valuable support always guide me in the right direction. You are a creative force, and anyone who knows you appreciates your wisdom, talent, fire, and enthusiasm. I will always treasure the time we spend together laughing, collaborating, and creating.

Fellow members of Peggy McColl's Elite Circle of Influence, what a privilege to have been surrounded by such an incredible group of people. Being in your presence has been both inspiring and invigorating. Thank you for supporting me in my growth and encouraging me to move forward with my dream.

Bob Proctor, I am so full of gratitude to finally be in the presence of someone who could actually put into words what I have felt my entire life. You struck every nerve and every emotion. You are the epitome of study, and I want to thank you for your contribution to the world and for being such an inspiration in my life. Your words of wisdom resonate with me on a cellular level, and I am forever grateful to know you. Although this book started off as a letter to you, it became so much more.

Sandy Gallagher, you are the queen of visioneering. I see you, I hear you. I am soaring in gratitude for your presence in my life. You have touched my heart immensely. You had me at *hit send and lead with love.* Thank you for pouring yourself into the study of the mind and sharing your knowledge with the world. Your visioneering technique played a huge role in helping me fulfill the vision of my dream. You will always be a beautiful inspiring light in my life.

My deepest appreciation and gratitude is given to the members of Bob Proctor and Sandy Gallagher's Inner Circle. Thank you for your support and dedication in holding me accountable for achieving my goal. I will always cherish our time together.

Thank you to Patti Knoles for creating my gorgeous book cover. Your patience and kindness will always remain at the forefront of my mind when I gaze at my book.

Judy O'Beirn with Hasmark Publishing, thank you for taking me under your wing and always being that positive reinforcement in my life, reminding me that I've got this. You and your team of experts have been such a pleasure to work with.

Justin Spizman, award-winning and bestselling book architect, I am extremely grateful for your time, energy, patience, and superb attention to detail. I'm so glad I listened to my intuition and reached out to you when I did. You asked all the right questions and supported me with your guidance. You sparked a fire within and for this I am forever grateful. I am honored to know you and to have had the opportunity to work with you as your presence was a huge contribution to my book.

Through many tears and great laughter, I extend heartfelt gratitude to my study partners Julie Smithwick, Kevin D. Smith, Rosangela De Vincenzo, Matt De Vincenzo, Rachel Bazzy, Nicole Hibbard, and Lisa Hawkyard. Your presence has been instrumental in this endeavor. Together we have uncovered life-changing information, and I wouldn't trade it for anything in the world. We are profoundly connected. The world is certainly a better place because you are in it.

I feel honored to have so many amazing, supportive friends. It has been a humbling experience to receive such genuine love and enthusiasm from all of you both near and far. You have enriched my life immensely. Thank you for your kind words of encouragement through this entire process. When my light was dim, you loaned me yours. You let me bounce things off you and gave me honest feedback. You showered me with love and expressed how much you believed in me every time we spoke. Your willingness to be there for me has filled me with an overflowing stream of gratitude, and I will always remember the huge role each of you have played in my life.

Most importantly, I'd like to extend my heartfelt gratitude to my family, as they have been a major source of inspiration in my life. I am deeply grateful for my husband, Keefe Ditta. Thank you for believing in me even when I questioned my own belief at times. You have been such an amazing cheerleader. Your boundless love and unwavering support have enhanced my life forever. Marriage is a partnership, not a dictatorship. I am so proud that we support each other in our dreams and build upon them together. You are such an incredible man, and I love everything about you. Thank you to my wonderful children and their spouses, Josh Rojas (Danielle) and Kacie Gros (Derick). I am deeply moved by your sincere and loving support. You listened with compassion as I struggled to read and share sacred parts of my book through tears. Thank you for believing in me and always encouraging me to the finish line.

In memory of my son Ryan Ditta, who transitioned into the next phase of his eternal journey in early 2015. I am so grateful for the many life lessons that arose during our time together. I felt your presence during many hours of writing. Thank you for confirming certain topics and phrases. The forgiveness chapter belongs to you and me. You are so loved and will always remain in my heart.

As parents we believe that we are here to teach our children, when in fact our children are our greatest teachers. You have all been a reliable source of continued education and have taught me so much over the years. Every moment I get to spend with you is such a blessing. I love and appreciate all of you.

Thank you to my mother, Peggy Wingerter. You are my trusted confidant, and I am eternally grateful for all that you do. Thank you for your constant support, for always believing in me, and for being my number one fan while anxiously awaiting your copy of this book. Your excitement is a beautiful reminder of the boundless love you have bestowed upon me since the day I was born. I love you so much, and I am so proud to be your daughter.

Thank you to my sister and brother-in-law, Jaimie and Matt Crook, for your constant love and support in all of my crazy endeavors. I cherish the bond we have. Jaimie, I love having you for a sister, and I love having Matt as a bonus brother. I am so grateful for all of our conversations about life, love, family, and investments. Whether you realize this or not, you are both a huge inspiration to me, and I love you dearly.

And finally, to my brother, Henry Huber, I love you so much. You always have a cheerful smile and an abundance of love in your heart. Your happy-go-lucky attitude toward life is what makes you so special to me. I am so grateful for your love and supportive words of encouragement. You always seemed to call and check in on me at the right time. No matter how many miles are between us, I will always carry you in my heart of hearts.

TABLE OF CONTENTS

FOREWORD

Wendy and Keefe Ditta were clients of mine, and then they became friends. And they're good friends. When Wendy asked me if I would write the foreword for her book, I was more than happy to.

The Ditta's have attended numerous seminars over the past few years and, unlike a lot of people who come to our programs; they were not seeking success. They were already doing very well with a hugely successful business that they had been operating for a number of years. But they knew that regardless of how well they were doing, they weren't doing much relative to what they were really capable of doing. Unfortunately, that's a truth of life that many people who enjoy some success never really learn.

Wendy has done a remarkable job of organizing the information and lessons that she has learned. And as Napoleon Hill would put it, she has intelligently directed that information in the book that you now hold in your hands. She has a beautiful way of expressing and getting her points across.

Let's take a moment and look at what Wendy has done with what she's learned. The title of the book really tells it all, "*The More I Learn, The More I Love.*"

When we think of learning, what we're really doing is expanding our level of awareness, our consciousness ... which is really the secret to life. Love is resonance. When two people are in love, they have a rapport on an intellectual level, they also have a rapport on an emotional or spiritual level which then leads to a strong, healthy, physical relationship.

When people are in love with what they're working on, they're intellectually, emotionally and physcially involved with their work. And, one of the beautiful truths of life is that work is made for us, we're not made for work. We should spend our days doing what we truly love to do.

As Wendy points out on the cover of her book, she is discovering the true beauty of life by reconnecting to self through love, light, and laughter. Everyone who knows Wendy would totally agree with that and would say, "Yes, that's Wendy." You can really benefit from the work she's done in this book and the way she's laid out the lessons she has learned.

Take a moment before you get into the book and ask yourself – if I were living the way I really want to live, what would my life look like? Take the time to answer that question and put it in writing. To move from where you are to the new life that you dream of, you will have to make a shift. Wendy helps you with that in the very first chapter of the book. She explains the laws of life in the second and third chapters – how exact they are and through the proper use of our mind, how we're capable of creating the life we want.

You're also going to discover that we're all conditioned ... we have a program in our mind that somebody else created and it's controlling how we spend our days. That program has to be rewritten which is exactly what Wendy Ditta has done in her own life. Step by step she explains how it has worked for her and by following the same path, it will work for you.

This is not a speed test to see how fast you can move into this new lifestyle. Rather it's something that you can work at daily, and thoroughly enjoy the experience along the way. I can assure you, before you finish the last chapter, you're going to be very grateful that Wendy has taken the time to share how she has moved into this magical way of living. You're also going to become aware that gratitude is an attitude that improves everything.

As you work through the book, page to page, chapter to chapter, keep in mind that no amount of reading or mentoring will improve your life. It is the understanding and the application of the ideas that you're about to read that actually causes everything to happen.

My wish for you is that you gain as much from the information that Wendy has shared in this book as Wendy Ditta has.

Bob Proctor, Teacher in the Secret and Best-Selling Author of *You Were Born Rich*

INTRODUCTION

"Row, row, row your boat gently down the stream, merrily, merrily, merrily, merrily life is but a dream." Do you recognize this familiar children's song? I remember singing it over and over again as a child, yet I was clueless of its true meaning. It wasn't until I started to question life and its true meaning that I began to wake up. Is life but a dream? If so, what is our human existence really all about? This great mystery has weighed heavily on my heart and mind for many years, especially because I felt like I lost myself while I seemed to drift aimlessly downstream.

Even though we are God's highest form of creation, I didn't feel worthy of that title. I felt like I simply existed, regressing in many ways if you will. I focused on doing the same things day in and day out with no real meaning. There was an absence of inner fulfillment, and I knew I wasn't living up to my potential. I just knew there had to be a deeper meaning to life than I experienced.

Thinking back, I clearly remember receiving nudges from God/ Source/Universe/Spirit throughout my life, but sadly I ignored them most of the time. I often allowed ego, fear, and frustration to take over rather than focus intently on the nudges and whispers edging me forward, thinking I knew best. So this time, while sitting in a seminar, when I heard a whisper to awaken to my truth and my existence, I decided to go all in on my spiritual journey. Ever surrender into the arms of someone you love? Well, that's exactly how it felt when I surrendered into the shift. Through my spiritual awakening a different way of thinking and experiencing life bubbled to the surface. It was the most beautiful feeling in the world. The first thing that comes to mind is love. It's all about love.

I experienced a longing and discontentment within for years. I used to joke about how my husband and I were the perfect couple because he was a workaholic and I was a shopaholic. I now see right through that statement. It's not as funny as it used to be. In fact, it's not funny at all. I fully recognize that I was just trying to fill a void in my life. My continuous search for contentment outside of myself always left me empty. Life is way too precious to lose ourselves in the things we do not love.

I often felt like there was an inner tug-of-war going on, and I knew that no matter how much grief, fear, sadness, or regret arose, running away from myself was not an option this time. I woke up to the realization that to reach the peace I was seeking, I had to endure the pain and stop running from it. It's as if my whole life had been revealed to me. Now I can clearly see where I was, where I currently am, and how I actively got here.

For years I put my dreams on the back burner through many forms of resistance such as fear, uncertainty, nonbelief in myself, excuses, and procrastination. Simply put, I was standing in my own way. My subconscious mind was infected with so many negative thoughts, and this caused me to behave in a way that was not consistent with my authentic self. From childhood onward, I suppressed hurtful feelings and slowly built a wall around myself – a wall I have spent the latter years of my life removing, brick by brick, in the form of shedding ego, clearing away old conditioned beliefs, and shifting lifelong paradigms. I can honestly say I feel as if I have been searching for myself forever, only now seeing a clear reflection.

When we don't feel good about ourselves we tend to tuck so much of ourselves away. I came to realize that when we do this we are only suppressing our gifts, which leads to suffering within as a natural consequence. We all possess valuable and unique gifts and talents. Be brave enough to share yours with the world. Your very being is a part of life expressing itself. So many are playing it small, and I was no exception. It was very difficult for me to break through the myopic perception I held of myself. Have you ever felt that way? Have you considered the gifts you may be suppressing? Do you have a longing to be more and do more with your life? Well then, it's time to end the longing and suffering.

As I became conscious of my mental entrapment, I was drawn to search for my truth. Through inner reflection I began to know myself at the core. In doing so, I absolutely knew that I was living a life that no longer resonated with my inner being. I also knew that if I wanted to pursue my dreams, ignite my potential, and live a life I loved, I had to embrace change. I started questioning everything just like a child would. *Why? Why am I doing what I am doing? What makes me think something is right or wrong? How did I come to this or that conclusion?* When the realization hits you that most of what you have been taught is false, your mind is bombarded with a tsunami of questions and thoughts.

To move forward I knew I had to give up something in order to get something. In this case I had to give up fear and surrender into the love and trust of the universe. In doing so I slowly reconnected to my authentic self by approaching life with a renewed sense of self, a heart full of gratitude, and an awakened spirit. Since coming home to my truest self I feel expanded by way of the dissolving dissonance. I learned how to use the hidden power within to create a life I loved. Living intentionally, creating positive changes in my life, and having a better understanding of forgiveness, gratitude, and love have also altered the way I view the world. I am more open to loving myself, loving others, loving life, and loving the universe without burden. Because of the astounding love that has encompassed me, I have found tremendous growth in my spiritual connection with God. I see it as strength. I have never felt such a divine connection as I do today.

Life teaches many lessons, but do you see them? Do you hear them? Do you feel them? Open yourself up to the nudges you may be receiving. I for one am not afraid of my truth any longer. Love has been my spiritual and mental nutrition. We are all on this journey of life together. Throughout this book I share some of my personal stories about how I turned ego, fear, and frustration into love. My shift in consciousness has altered my life in such a way that now allows for peace, love, harmony, and joy to surface and remain at the forefront of every day. Learning how to actively use my mind to create a life I love has been a gift of clarity.

Through my studies I have learned that I, and only I, have total control over my actions and emotions. I have also learned to rise above. My narrative will be your primer for doing the same. As this book unfolds you may begin to question many aspects of your own life. I sincerely hope that my experiences will somehow help you expand your thinking and bring forth a new clarity and understanding to your own personal journey.

My intention and hope is that this book will open a path for you to look within and bring forth an awareness and openness that leads you to the most authentic version of yourself. Living a fulfilled life is about doing what you love through authenticity and joy. Don't be afraid to dive deep within. In searching for a deeper understanding through spiritual expansion, I graciously share my vulnerability and deepest thoughts on how aligning my heart and mind have led to discovering the true beauty of life by reconnecting to self through love, light, and laughter.

ONE

SURRENDERING INTO THE SHIFT

Surrendering into the shift invites authenticity by causing you to go inward and relinquish the old identity by peeling away the many layers of sadness, brokenness, and any other form of powerlessness once believed to be true about yourself. Through surrender, you gradually gain control of your life, and what emerges is a more expanded self. Stepping into the new you and leaving the old you behind takes strength and courage. Through deep surrender you will come to experience life through a whole new lens. Priorities shift and the way you view others starts to change. As the perceived veils of brokenness lift, you will gain a whole new perspective on life – that is, your life in general – and you may feel compelled to lead with love in all areas of life.

Those who surrender into the shift will have the desire to pull away from anything that is no longer good for them. Questioning thoughts about one's existence begin to surface. There's a pull to do more in life in search of meaning. Little synchronicities become evident, causing one to pause and ponder. Many will reflect upon times in their lives when things went wrong, prompting a yearning to bring about more peace, love, and compassion in the world.

As the soul awakens during the shift to a new awareness, although very rewarding, it can be both painful and perplexing. So many new truths reveal themselves, causing one to experience deep emotional reactions. The awakening process can happen in an instant, but more than likely it will unfold over the course of many years. Although everyone is unique and no two awakening processes are the same, it would be quite difficult to convey exactly what happens when one finally wakes up.

My Journey to Self

I love to marvel at the midnight skies, taking in the vast beauty of magnificence, as it feels grand and beyond my comprehension. In 2012 a very memorable shift occurred in my life in the middle of the night while standing under the open sky. While stargazing, I experienced a moment of solitude like never before. The twinkling of the stars mesmerized me as I stared in wonder with a feeling of complete gratitude, knowing that it is a miracle just to be alive. I have often questioned my existence, wondering why I am here, and I'm struck by how incredible it is to think about how we are living on planet earth while simultaneously suspended in the universe with precision.

It doesn't matter how many times I revisit that thought, I still cannot seem to wrap my head around it. During that moment of solitude, I became aware of a conversation in my mind. Although I have experienced this my entire life, in that very moment it struck me as odd. Something happened on the inside of me as this incessant mind chatter carried on. It prompted a huge shift in my awareness. I became aware of my awareness, causing me to question, *If I am asking, then who is answering?* This was quite a mystery to me and one that I was not willing to abandon.

What I have learned is that there is so much more to our existence than what most consider. We are more than just a physical body; we are spiritual beings having a human experience. If you are the observer of your thoughts, then you can't be your thoughts. Self-realization is when you realize that you are in fact not your body, you *have* a body, and that you are not your thoughts, you are the observer of your thoughts. That intriguing moment of self-realization has remained with me ever since. Experiencing a shift in consciousness caused me to start questioning everything in my life. I began to think about how my entire life has been shaped by my thoughts. Shrugging it off did not appeal to me as I clearly sensed that something within was seeking freer, fuller expansion. Hence my journey to self. I told no one at the time. It was a very real and personal experience that I needed to explore. I felt an extreme urgency to be alone and analyze my life. It was evident that something very profound was unfolding, and continues to do so today.

Mental Mind Chatter

Have you ever noticed your own mind chatter and how it never seems to shut down? In my experience of self-realization, the one asking and the one answering are one and the same. You can actually have a full-blown argument in your mind and no one will know the difference. Ever try to fall asleep, but you have so much on your mind that you can't? This incessant mind chatter will keep you preoccupied for hours, causing you to toss and turn. It will interfere with your ability to think straight at times. It's exhausting! It can jump to a conclusion faster than a speeding bullet. I remember enjoying a wonderful serene massage, and the next thing I knew I had my entire month planned out. Have you ever driven home, but because you were so preoccupied by your thoughts you didn't even remember driving home?

Surrendering into the shift encourages one to calm the mind. Many use meditation or breathing methods; some practice yoga, while others find journaling helps. The body is the instrument of the mind. Worry and overthinking can cause physical illness in the body. Although we have been gifted with a higher faculty of imagination, we have been taught to use our imagination in the wrong way. If we constantly worry, then we are constantly adding stress to our bodies. Stress arises from being obsessed with negative memories, feelings, thoughts, and emotions, and the vast majority of them are of no importance to begin with. Calming the mind is the only way out. We must shift our thinking and regain control over our thoughts.

The Wall of Insecurity

I have always been a very loving, caring, and thoughtful person. But as a constant people-pleaser, I actively denied my own needs and feelings. I remember listening to the conversations in my mind since I was a child. They have always been there; I just didn't realize I didn't have to believe everything I thought. I didn't know I was separate from my thoughts. My incessant mind chatter caused me to suppress hurtful feelings and hide behind a wall of insecurity. As I grew older, my insecurities also grew. In time I managed to subconsciously build a solid wall around myself. This wall was built in the form of ego, conditioning, and paradigms. I jokingly, but seriously, refer to that wall as Gangsta Wendy. Yes! I named my alter ego. Normally, having a tough exterior would not be considered a bad thing, but hiding behind a bad attitude is—and that only added layers to the wall I used to separate myself from the outside world. I blocked emotions and lost touch with who I was, making it nearly impossible for me to truly let anyone in. It was all ego.

The thoughts I listened to on a continuous basis were ingrained in my subconscious mind and eventually became my life. My repeat loop of mind chatter went something like this: *You are not deserving of all good things. Who do you think you are? You aren't worthy. You're not smart enough. You're not good enough. Your opinion doesn't matter. You are invisible. No one really cares about you. You're too fat. You're too thin. You're way too tall. You laugh too loud. You're not important. You don't have anything important to share.*

Those thoughts were deeply embedded, and because ego is the driving force behind our subconscious triggers, ego made a grand entrance every single day to keep me right where I was, feeling defeated before I even began. Our feelings and emotions don't just magically disappear into the ether. That energy has to go somewhere. Namely it shows up in the body. It is either processed and released or unprocessed and suppressed deep within. That suppressed energy will permeate every cell of your body until you forgive it or detach yourself from it.

A Pivotal Moment

We've been programmed to find happiness externally in people, places, and things. It doesn't surprise me that there is so much debt and unhappiness in the world today. The joy of living comes from within. You cannot live an empowered life if you continue to look outside of yourself for validation. I am so thankful I came to that realization when I heard a whisper that led me searching within. Seems I had forgotten about that quiet sacred space, and I am so grateful I listened to that marvelous whisper. The whisper was far different from the incessant mind chatter I experienced on a daily basis. This whisper was a still small voice, angelic, soft, and serene. Since surrendering into the shift, I humbly share with you how honesty and love have been the foundation of the relationship I now have with myself. Without these two beautiful virtues my self-discovery never would have been found.

In early 2014, I attended a seminar by Proctor Gallagher Institute called The Science of Getting Rich. During the seminar, Sandy Gallagher spoke about gratitude, love, and joy and how we should implement those virtues into our daily lives. She taught that we should each *send love* (emanating from our mind) to the people who bother us most. This brought happy tears to my eyes because it was right in line with how I was living my life, having declared new beginnings just a few years prior. I was at first taken aback by the part where you are supposed to send love to those who bother you because even though I considered myself a good person, I wasn't sure if I could actually do that.

So I fiercely fought the thought. *Nope! No way! Those people do not deserve my love.* But then Sandy explained that it wasn't for the other person. It was for me. Sending love to those who bother you most will free you from hatred. It will free you from being held hostage by your own negative thoughts. It's all a part of the shift. We all want peace, but most people choose not to release the negative energy they have stored up inside of them seemingly giving them rank over the other person or situation. But by releasing those thoughts, you are creating world peace and introducing a sense of calmness to your very existence. You are creating world peace in the world you live in, the environment you have created.

In the past I had a wall up so high to protect my precious ego, and I was always dressed in my tough girl armor ready to face anyone at any time. So one of the first people I sent love to that day at the seminar was myself. With what felt like a million emotions clamoring inside of me, I just couldn't hold it in any longer, and I started to cry with my husband on one side of me and my son on the other. Everything Bob and Sandy were saying resonated with me on a cellular level, like: let go and let God, lead with love, remain in a good vibration, serve others, be a good little giver, and hit send. Yes! Hit send and move in the direction of the life that makes you happiest.

That's exactly what I wanted, and the more they spoke, the more the tears flowed. That seminar wasn't just about setting a bunch of goals and learning how to earn more money, it was about shifting into the highest version of yourself. The entire seminar hit me like a ton of bricks. It was such a pivotal moment in my life. Talk about a lightbulb moment. It all goes hand in hand.

I sat there frozen while a tremendous amount of emotional pain surfaced. The thought of running away from myself was not an option this time. As difficult as it is to break through the bondage of ego, I knew I was not going to let it win this time. I encountered the painful realization that to reach the peace I was seeking, I had to endure the pain and stop running from it. There was no turning back. Who wants to go back? Go back to what? Just existing? Not me, not ever. I was ready to move in the direction of a life that made me happiest. It was time to come face-to-face with the egoic powers that had held me captive for so long and caused me to build a wall of protection around myself since I was a child. It was time to be free.

Everything Bob and Sandy spoke about was exactly what I had been striving for, and I was sick to my stomach when I realized I had spent years pursuing that version of myself only to find out I was doing it half-assed. The truth was staring me right in the face: I was afraid to remove the wall. It didn't matter if I had perfected all the things they were speaking about or not. Without removing the wall, I would *never* shift into the highest version of myself. No one would. I had to get out of my own head! That is where any shift begins – replacing anger, fear, and frustration with love. By doing so you remove the barriers in every form that have prevented your expansion of growth and connection to others. As obvious as it may seem now, removing the wall was the missing piece of information I needed to shed in order to shift my life as a whole.

My ego didn't want anyone to see my weaknesses or vulnerability, and as crazy as this may sound, I didn't even know who I was without my wall of protection, but it was time to remove it all. As soon as I exhaled and my body relaxed, I heard a still small voice repeatedly whisper, *Awaken to your truth and existence.* So many thoughts raced through my mind. I thought exposing my weaknesses would be a sign of weakness. But as I leaned into a greater depth of understanding, I later realized it was actually a sign of strength and courage.

I did it! I had myself at hello as I stepped wholeheartedly into who I am. I surrendered into the shift, releasing all the built-up resistance that bound me from authenticity. I felt the wall of torment falling away from me. My force awakened, and all the hurtful feelings I'd held onto for so long diminished and were replaced with an abundance of love. I was awash in benevolence. I loved who I discovered, and the most important part of all is that it didn't matter to me one iota what anyone else thought. It was a new way of being, being my authentic self. What a freeing experience.

A Gentle Force of Knowing

Be brave enough to explore the depth of who you are. When you start to change on the inside, everything else on the outside follows suit. I knew I was on the right path because of the overwhelming feeling of love and gratitude that encompassed me. It was a gentle force of knowing, and my senses opened up like I had never experienced before. I welcomed and honored the shift, as it has opened my heart and mind to places deep within that I didn't even know existed. There is infinite depth in being present in the moment, experiencing it, savoring it, inhaling it, and, most importantly, surrendering to it. Because I surrendered into the shift for the first time in my life, I can honestly say *I feel alive*. I say this with a deep knowing and divine spiritual connection to God/Source/Universe/Spirit. Knowing transcends both belief and faith; it is purely an experience.

I no longer have the unpleasant need to feel so guarded against my rightful place in the universe, and I no longer live in spiritual poverty. Today I honor the life rising up inside of me, and I direct my energy toward living my best life. We are here to love, grow, and expand. I questioned how I could have had a different perspective on life. It's like, where in the world have I been all my life? I have learned that the treasure house is within. I began to seek answers with a clear mind and an open heart with no preconceptions.

A New Direction of Bliss

I started to have clarity on the daily choices I faced by understanding the power of my thoughts and the effect they have had over my entire life. As I moved forward with courage, grace, and a soul that sparkled, I was happier and had an overwhelming sense of peace and gratitude. My life has been catapulted in a new direction of bliss.

Changing the way I saw others and myself has been a beautiful new discovery. Once I understood the power of my thoughts and just how powerful and effective the subconscious mind is, it made sense to choose genuine, loving, and kind thoughts every day. Surrendering into the shift allowed me to shed Gangsta Wendy and all of her outdated beliefs and enabled the Goddess in her to energetically and effectively shine through. I may have mastered many things but fell significantly short on others. It has taken many years and tears to get to where I am today. Like many, I am still a work in progress. And while I respect my own progress, I am just as respectful of others'.

Since surrendering into the shift I have an undeniable urge to share love daily in all the things I do and say. How could I have been so off-course for so long? Conditioning? Yes. I let my conditions and my circumstances dictate who I thought I should or should not be. I was clearly living a life fully *unaware* of who I was. I wandered around aimlessly like so many others, being weighed down by the day-to-day practices of what I thought was the meaning of life. Life is such a beautiful gift. No one is here by accident. We all have a chosen path, an intentional direction. But do you know what your direction is?

A Journey of Love

Although I am not proud of the way I behaved at times in the past, the beauty in what I have learned has ultimately changed my life. It has opened my eyes to see through a new lens of life. For so long I identified myself as my ego, Gangsta Wendy, but I've learned that ego is just an illusion of who we think we are. Waking up to who you really are causes you to release the idea of who you imagined yourself to be. As you surrender into the shift or shift into a higher version of yourself, your life begins to transform and so does everything around you. The shift is a journey of love by way of shedding your ego and removing all the barriers to reveal your true self. When you're ready to release the walls of protection, your heart will be at ease and your life will be enhanced with love. Envelop yourself in the magnificence of life and authenticity.

We each have a divine spiritual essence within, and this book will help you reconnect to that spiritual essence thereby revealing the true beauty of life. Shifting into a higher version of yourself is the first step in inviting authenticity, peace, love, and joy into your life. Are you ready to make a shift? If so, this book is for you. Be sure to review the Loving Reminders at the end of each chapter, as they may serve as powerful reference points.

Loving Reminders

- ♥ Through surrender you gain control over your life.
- ♥ Surrendering into the shift encourages one to calm the mind.
- ♥ You are so much more than just a physical body.
- ♥ You are not your body, you have a body.
- ♥ You are not your thoughts, you are the observer of your thoughts.
- ♥ The joy of living comes from within.
- ♥ Sending love to those who bother you most will free you from being held hostage from your own negative thoughts.
- ♥ Be brave enough to explore the depth of who you are.
- ♥ We are here to love, grow, and expand.
- ♥ We all have a spiritual essence within.

TWO

UNIVERSAL LAWS:
THE KEYS TO GREAT SUCCESS

Whether you surrender into the shift through a spiritual awakening or purposefully shift into a higher version of yourself, outside factors that once influenced your happiness and well-being subside and are replaced with a more meaningful and happy existence. I personally became more aware of my life and the environment in which I existed mentally, physically, spiritually, financially, and relationally. I wanted to create a life that I was truly proud of living. That meant creating a life I loved on the inside, not just one that looked great on the outside.

As Bob Proctor began to speak about the universal laws, I sat in the audience captivated. In that moment, I realized and subscribed to the notion that a number of very real and remarkably powerful laws are at work in the background of our lives. These invisible laws impact us, fulfill us, and maintain a great presence in the way we choose to live. God is the creator, and the laws are God's words in action. As Bob continued to speak, his words not only prompted a huge shift in my life, they also helped me realize how I was in fact using the universal laws. If we are to shift our lives, we have to be aware and willing to interact with these laws, as they are the keys to great success and living a harmonious life of abundance.

As my studies continued I learned that we unknowingly invite additional challenges into our lives through our thoughts, so I purposely set out to change my way of thinking. How often have you manifested negative results in your life because of negative thoughts? Wouldn't you rather manifest healthy, wealthy, and more favorable results? Learn to accept an abundant life in your own mind even if you don't believe it is so right now. Thoughts become things as the result of an immutable law, and by understanding this I am now fully aware of and take careful inventory of what I think about. It is purely by awareness that one is able to use this law in one's favor.

Now, whether you realize this or not, we have all been using these laws our entire lives in one way or another, yet some have used them more effectively than others. You simply cannot plant negative thoughts and expect a positive outcome. Be mindful that just as certain as you plant corn you will reap corn. It's the law! Because your subconscious mind is like that of a garden, what you faithfully plant will faithfully grow.

The next step on our journey forward is understanding that these laws have always been an integral part of who you are. As you do so, you will begin to live more freely, purposefully, and successfully. The laws make sense, and as you learn how to integrate them confidently into your daily life through understanding, you will begin to create deliberate change in your life. Your thoughts and actions will be fueled with purpose and meaningful direction rather than aimless yearning.

To help you, I've included several laws that assisted me in my journey as well as a brief summary of each for your reference. As you increase your awareness of both their existence and interaction with your world, you can become more aware of these laws and start to implement them as a part of your personal shift.

The Universal Laws of Existence

Law of Vibration: The Law of Vibration tells us that everything moves, and nothing rests. Just look around you; everything in the universe is vibrating. Although you cannot see the things around you moving, they are. If you place any item under a microscope you will see movement in the mass. Higher levels of consciousness produce a higher level of vibration. For example, a desk or chair doesn't vibrate at the same frequency as a human being. Everything has its own vibrational frequency. Thoughts, feelings, and actions emit a vibration. Good thoughts emit a positive vibration, and bad thoughts emit a negative one. Repetitive thoughts are embedded in the subconscious mind, and those thoughts being your dominant thought process become your dominant vibration. Your vibration will attract others on the same frequency. This is where the Law of Attraction comes in as the secondary law to the Law of Vibration, which is considered to be the primary law.

Law of Attraction: The basic premise of the Law of Attraction is *like* attracts *like*. It is the secondary law of the Law of Vibration. The Law of Attraction, when backed with action, is the ability to attract into your life whatever you focus on depending upon the vibration attached to it. Simply put, thoughts become things. Every area of your life is influenced by this law. By having the desire for something, you set in motion a line of energy toward it, and the expectation of it is what will attract it into your life. It is not magic, but it will seem magical when you begin to enjoy all the essential goodness it brings forth. It is the basic law of all manifestation. So don't ever desire something that you don't expect to appear in your life because that is just wishful thinking. And never expect something that you don't desire because you may just receive it.

Law of Cause and Effect: This law tells us that nothing happens by chance. For every action there is an equal and opposite reaction. The Law of Cause and Effect is also known as *karma*. Every cause has its effect, and every effect has its cause, which directly influences our existence. The entire universe is in perpetual motion. Good thoughts and actions create positive effects. Every thought, action, or deed performed sets in motion through vibrational thought energy chains of cause and effect. Many will use the word karma when they feel someone has wronged them. You'll hear them say, "Karma is a bitch." Then they sit back and wait for something bad in return to happen to the person who stepped in it. Karma is also positive. You get back what you put out, and that includes the good too. It's the boomerang effect. I just find it interesting that most people focus on how karma is a bitch when the truth is it isn't, it just *is*. It is whatever you make it. It is whatever you put out into the world. I'd also like to share that by waiting and expecting karma to get back at the other person, you are only opening yourself up to negative energy. Don't even concern yourself with those thoughts.

Law of Belief: The Law of Belief tells us that whatever we believe, with feeling enforced behind the belief, becomes our reality. We've been conditioned to think that seeing is believing, but the Law of Belief is simply *believing* is seeing. Your belief system supports your thoughts, and your thoughts are connected to the *feeling of belief* in oneself. Your belief creates your reality. Do you believe you will have financial success, or do you believe that you will not have financial success? Do you believe that you will meet the partner of your dreams, or do you believe that you will not meet the partner of your dreams? Create a life you love by utilizing the Law of Belief.

Law of Compensation: The Law of Compensation tells us that, without fail, it will bear unto you the equivalent in return to what you do, what you think, and what you give. When most people first hear of this law they think only in monetary terms. It is so much more than that. If you want to earn more money, then you must increase the value of your contribution. If you fill your mind with negative thoughts, it will compensate you with anger, frustration, resentment, fear, anxiety, and so forth. What you feed your mind will be served right back to you. Feed it beautiful happy thoughts of success, gratitude, love, joy, and forgiveness, and a harmonious state of well-being will be your compensation. The amount of money you earn will always be in ratio to the need for what you do, the ability to do it, and the difficulty there is in replacing you. Always do more than what you have been paid to do no matter who is watching. So many want to make certain their efforts have been noticed, but that's just the ego. Do more, and by doing it from the heart the unseen forces will reward you in unexpected ways. Those who expect to get something for nothing are working against the law.

Law of Relativity: The Law of Relativity tells us that it is anything in comparison to. All things are relative. It is only our thinking that makes something big or small, high or low, light or dark, good or bad. Many people have expressed that they have big problems in life. Compared to what? It isn't a big problem (or a small problem); it is just a problem, but our thinking is what makes it big (or small). It all depends on how you identify with it.

Law of Non-Resistance: The Law of Non-Resistance tells us that the universe is always conspiring with us to bring about resources to help fulfill our many dreams and desires. But when we resist people, places, and things that we do not care for with our thinking, we are actually feeding the resistance even more power. Forcing negates and is ineffective in acquiring your dreams. Have you ever wanted something so badly in your life, and then once you stopped trying to force it to happen it suddenly appeared? How many couples have tried so hard to get pregnant and couldn't, but once they adopted a baby they ended up getting pregnant. It's because they stopped forcing it. In school my teacher made us write out, *I will not talk during class.* Well, guess what we continued to do? Talk during class. The assignment should have been, *I will be respectful in class.* What you resist persists.

Law of Receiving: The Law of Receiving tells us that there is a constant flow of energy through giving and receiving. For the law to work effectively in your life you must be able to give and receive freely. Willingly give and graciously receive. You have a choice in what circulates in your life. Giving and receiving keeps the abundance of the universe circulating in our lives. Continue to give even if those you help do not reciprocate. By giving from the heart, the universe will return your effort at a time when you least expect it. Many think they will give once they receive, but this is not how the law works. You must give in order to receive.

Law of Supply: The Law of Supply tells us there is constant growth and an unlimited source of everything you will ever need. This divine energy is the source of all abundance. Everything has already been given to us; it is up to us to come into harmony with what we desire in order to receive it. There is no such thing as not enough or too much. Supply does not come from one main channel, it may come from many. Your only job is to be aware that it is coming your way with great expectancy. The only way you can block abundance in your life is by focusing on lack. You must abolish the thoughts of lack to be in sync with the supply of abundance that is readily available to you. You can have as much of anything as you want because, like all of creation, you were designed to live in abundance. The soul is content but never satisfied, for it is always searching for freer, fuller expansion.

Law of Polarity: The Law of Polarity tells us that everything has a dual nature. Everything expresses itself in the polar opposite. It exists so that we may experience life fully with the understanding that without cold there could be no hot, and without a left there could be no right, and without an up there could be no down. Opposites are identical in nature but different in degree. We experience all of these. The Law of Polarity works hand in hand with the Law of Attraction. While these two laws are separate, they work together to influence your manifestation potential. The Law of Attraction is *like attracts like* while the Law of Polarity is *opposites attract*.

Law of Increase: The Law of Increase tells us that if you want more of anything in your life then you must praise what you already have. Give gratitude for all the love, health, money, energy, friends, and so forth that are in your life. There is an infinite supply and it is all available to you. Praise everyone and everything. Give sincere compliments, smile, be polite, and open doors. Leaving people with an impression of increase not only adds value to their lives, but it changes their vibration and will of course enhance yours. When you praise children watch how they thrive. The same holds true for plants. It's not by chance, it's by law. If you form contractive thoughts of fear and criticism, you are working against the law.

Law of Forgiveness: The Law of Forgiveness tells us that we must be forgiving of others if we wish to be on the receiving end of forgiveness. Forgiveness allows you to be in harmony with the law of your being. Because forgiveness releases negative energies, it ensures healing. The natural result will be peace of mind, body, and spirit. Forgiveness will allow you to reap the benefit of moving forward without the negative attachment of thought.

Law of Sacrifice: The Law of Sacrifice states that you cannot get something you want without giving up something in return. When one commonly hears of the word sacrifice they think only of giving up something, but the law states that sacrifice is giving up something in order to get something. For example, sacrifice your laziness to create the life you truly desire. Think of the athletes, dancers, and musicians who have sacrificed time with family and friends to pursue their dreams of being champions in their field. There is always a price to pay for what you want in life.

Law of Obedience: The Law of Obedience tells us that we are building our lives either in wisdom or ignorance, depending upon the direction of obedience. While we follow this Law of Obedience, we welcome into our lives happiness and peace. If you obey a negative lifestyle, you will indeed receive a negative life. As you obey the law, the proof will be in your results. Pay attention to what you are building in your life through your daily habits.

Law of Gestation: The Law of Gestation tells us that there is a natural order to things. Everything in the universe is bound by law. Just as a human baby gestates in the womb for nine months, any form of creation has a gestation period. The dreams we hold so near and dear to our hearts also have a necessary gestation period, the only difference is no one knows the gestation of bringing a dream into manifestation. There is a time and a season for everything. Cultivate patience and trust the process.

Law of Perpetual Transmutation: The Law of Perpetual Trans-mutation tells us that change is all there is. We all have the power to change our lives by the images we hold in our minds. Energy moves into form, through form, and then back into form. It is always in motion and never remains still. This formless energy is being shaped by your thoughts. As you harness this energy, you have the power within to transform it into whatever you choose. This is what happens when you pray. Through positive thoughts, you can manifest change.

Law of Reflection: The Law of Reflection says that what you see and condemn in others reflects what you see within yourself. Life itself becomes a mirror for self-knowledge; everyone is reflecting a part of who you are. This universal mirror can be very humbling, and it may be difficult to digest, but once you understand what the Law of Reflection is teaching, your spiritual growth will expand. It can be brutally honest, and as long as you are willing to learn, the lessons will reveal themselves. When you see a certain characteristic in someone, whether good or bad, the soul is trying to get you to see that reflection in yourself. Oftentimes people are quick to point out the negative in others without even noticing or acknowledging the negative within themselves.

Law of Gratitude: The Law of Gratitude states that whenever you are grateful it raises your vibrational frequency and supports your getting in harmony with the energy of the universe. By acknowledging and giving sincere thanks for everything in your life, you are opening a pathway for more. No matter how bad life seems, there is always, always something to be grateful for.

The Laws in Action

Each of these laws governs and impacts our lives, either directly or indirectly. They exist independent of whether we recognize them. Think about this: we're all familiar with electricity, right? Well, an invisible Law of Electricity is at work in the background of our lives too. This law governs the flow of electricity and generates light wherever you direct it, as long as it remains connected to its source. And, just like the universal laws, the Law of Electricity works with precision and applies to everyone who uses it. If you misuse it, you lose. The Law of Electricity didn't just magically appear over one hundred years ago, it has *always* been here. It wasn't until someone discovered how to use the law that we were able to enjoy all the benefits of it.

Although we may not physically be able to view the mind, we can certainly view the results of the mind through seeing that our thoughts, actions, attitudes, and intentions are responsible for shaping our lives. An example of this is found in the following story, which outlines the Law of Cause and Effect and how it never fails to show up in your life.

In September 2015, my friend John asked if I would host a fortieth birthday party for his wife, Shannon. I agreed and the party planning began. One of our biggest concerns was the cake. With Shannon owning her own bakery, we couldn't possibly ask her to bake her own cake. Or could we? Well, after many laughs and several phone calls, John and I decided it would be really funny if we could figure out a way to get Shannon to bake her own birthday cake.

John persuaded one of Shannon's regular customers to call in with a last-minute cake order. Shannon, feeling sorry for her seemingly desperate customer, reluctantly agreed to accept the order. The customer ordered a simple round two-tiered cake with purple and white icing and almond flavoring. Once the cake was taken care of, all the other planning seemed to fall right into place. The invitations went out, and behind the scenes we were sneaking around planning for the perfect surprise.

On the day of the party, the house was decorated, the food was catered, and since John was Shannon's number one delivery guy, he delivered the cake to me safe and sound earlier that afternoon. The guests started to arrive and anxiously awaited the arrival of the birthday girl. Someone yelled, "She's here!" We shushed each other and scattered all over the place. When Shannon walked through the front door, we yelled, "Surprise!" Everyone blew horns, laughed, smiled, and began taking pictures. Shannon was surprised as she made her way through the foyer, hugging all her guests. She let out an unexpected scream when she recognized certain people that she hadn't seen in years. When our eyes met, she said, "I hate surprises. I can't believe you surprised me!"

John and I laughed in anticipation while she continued greeting her guests, still posing for more pictures, this time with her husband and children. Finally, she made her way into the kitchen. Her eyes zeroed in on the cake like a magnet. I could see her wheels spinning. We all waited for her reaction. She laughed and screamed and laughed some more and said, "I cannot believe you got me to make my own cake! This cake is going to taste horrible. Seriously! I didn't add any almond flavoring! I was so aggravated when I received the order for this cake and look what happened!" While laughing, she said, "I can't get away from this cake!"

Shannon said yes to the customer although she wanted to say no. She proceeded to bake the cake with the wrong attitude. She felt frustrated, aggravated, and annoyed at herself for saying yes. On a normal less hectic day, she would have been cheerfully baking cakes, doing what she loves because she wanted to, not because she felt obligated to. But from the time she took the order, she knew she was not going to give that particular cake the attention it needed.

Because Shannon's mind was tainted, so became the cake. That cake didn't stand a chance! Well, Shannon declared that in the future she would only bake cakes with love or she wouldn't bake them at all.

Shannon might not have considered the Law of Cause and Effect in her response, but it was absolutely present and at work. Everything happens by law. In her actions, Shannon was unconsciously working against the Law of Cause and Effect. You simply cannot plant negativity and reap positivity. Hence, "Whatsoever a man soweth, that he shall also reap." Oftentimes people will do and say things without even thinking about the consequences. Had she maintained a better awareness of this law and embedded it into her life as the norm, she might have baked the best cake she could.

Align, Harmonize, and Utilize

The truth is you don't change your life by doing certain things, you change it by doing things in a certain way. That certain way is through following the principles and laws of the universe. It's just the surface scratch of your paradigm shift, but it is a needed crucial breakthrough to move in the direction of your dreams, goals, and aspirations. Do you doubt that you are entitled to all good things? Well, the universal laws say differently. Once you grasp even a basic understanding of how to properly utilize these laws, you can begin to create a fuller, richer, and more joyous life. It won't be necessary for you to knock on wood when great things happen in your life, as they're supposed to. When you understand how the creative law of your own mind works you will no longer blame others for the situations or conditions in your life; you will need only to look within. Educate yourself, study these laws, and apply them throughout your very existence. By learning how to align, harmonize, and utilize these laws, you will begin to transform your life by creating your intended reality.

Loving Reminders:

♥ These laws impact us, fulfill us, and maintain a great presence in the way in which we choose to live.

♥ God is the creator, and the laws are God's words in action.

♥ Thoughts become things.

♥ You simply cannot plant negative thoughts and expect a positive outcome.

♥ Each of these laws governs and impacts our lives, either directly or indirectly.

♥ The laws operate with precision and apply to everyone.

♥ You don't change your life by doing certain things, you change it by doing things in a certain way.

♥ You are entitled to all good things.

THREE

THE POWER OF THE MIND

As you implement the universal laws, also known as the laws of the mind, you will begin to see through the walls of ordinary life. You will also notice a substantial change in the way you think, interact with others, conduct business, and even relate to yourself. As my studies continued I learned more about the power of the mind through our six higher faculties, which are imagination, intuition, will, memory, reason, and perception. The more I learned, the more I wanted to learn. I simply couldn't get enough.

Many are unfamiliar with the workings of the power of the mind and how it can actually assist them in achieving great success. What you are about to discover in this chapter sets us humans apart from all other species. Humans have the conscious freedom of mind while animals act on instinct. Oh! And when was the last time you heard of a dog or a cat inventing something new through the imagination of thought?

The Wisdom of Life Is Awareness

The first step in learning how to utilize the power of the mind is developing self-awareness. Although it is far beyond the body, emotions, or thought process, it is not separate from you. You need not be in search of it, only develop it. Because we lose ourselves inside of our own self-image, what matters most is that you identify the wall that you have surrounded yourself with and why. The wisdom of life is awareness. It's the only way you will begin to move forward. It isn't until you become aware of your thoughts, emotions, and behavior that you are equipped to make the necessary changes toward a better direction in life. As you immerse yourself and become aware of such consciousness you are better able to change the interpretation of the mind and utilize its power.

Bob Proctor teaches on the seven levels of awareness as the following:

1. **Animal:** You allow your current circumstances to dictate your life. You react through fight or flight. You react instead of respond.

2. **Masses:** You follow the crowd rather than think for yourself. You prefer to conform rather than be in a creative state. Your paradigms rule you.

3. **Aspiration:** You desire something greater. After following the crowd for years, you recognize something inside of you craves more. Many will find themselves stuck at this level because they never apply action behind the desire. Wishing isn't willing.

4. **Individual:** You begin to express your uniqueness. But as you move forward your paradigms pull you back into your comfort zone. You end up back at level 2. Of course, your desire is still there but you remain stuck.

5. **Discipline:** At this point you realize that the only way to move forward is by giving yourself a command and following it.

6. **Experience:** Your actions change your results due to the experience you've gained through discipline. You now realize that you have a hidden power within.

7. **Mastery:** You respond rather than react. You begin to think and plan, as you are no longer controlled by old paradigms that once held you back.

I remained stuck at level 4 for many years. I had a longing and discontent to be, do, have, and give more in life, but I continued to replay the same worn-out record of disbelief in my mind over and over. The struggle was real. I didn't have any faith in myself or my dreams. I simply justified where I was in my life at that time. I put every dream I have ever had on the back burner all because of fear and disbelief.

You see, the freedom in living an authentic life is understanding the power of the mind through self-awareness. Because the conscious mind is awareness, we must learn to become more aware of ourselves. Until you do, you will continue to live in the same made-up stories of your mind. Your negative internal dialogue will continue to enhance your self-limiting patterns. As you forge ahead, I've also included a few questions for you to consider on your path to developing self-awareness:

1. Have you been completely honest with yourself and others?

2. Do you have a realistic and absolute understanding of your characteristics, qualities, and behavior?

3. Would others describe you the same way you describe yourself?

4. Do you behave differently in private than you do in public?

No matter your results, each of us harbors hidden issues within that will at some point need to be addressed. Immerse yourself into living in your answers to each of these questions. Give them great thought and honor yourself by being honest with your answers. The truth is you cannot change what you are not willing to acknowledge or admit to, so notice when the basic instinct of your ego presents itself as you answer these questions. Notice how ego has a powerful influence over your thoughts. Honesty is key to authenticity, growth, and self-awareness.

The Source of Power Is Within

Because we have been programmed as servants of the rational mind since childhood, we tend to communicate with the outside world by relying upon our outer sensory factors. By using them, we can see, hear, taste, touch, and smell. Although these sensory abilities are important, and you use them every day, you may be misled when you only rely on these senses. That's because things are not always as they seem.

The higher faculties of the intellect are quite extraordinary, and the mind can perform many functions. The activity of the mind is thought, and your thoughts absolutely create your environment. There is a life force behind your creative power. You must understand that you are a creative being working with an infinite universe, an infinite Power. God can only do for you what he can do through you. Once you develop a more heightened awareness of the power of the mind through your six higher faculties, outlined below, you will understand that your source of power is within. Simply allow the essence of Life to rise to the surface. Once you do, you will realize that you have been well equipped all along to create an extraordinary life. Many people believe they are not capable of living an extraordinary life, and so they feel dismayed and singled out. They are relying on an outside source to help them. The true Source is within. It's within all of us.

Everything you see on the physical plane began with the imagination of thought. It all begins with the imagination of thought. It wasn't until someone used their imagination to create devices like cell phones or cars that we were able to use them. The only reason we didn't have cell phones or cars hundreds of years ago is because no one thought of them. The material to build them has always been here; it only required someone using their imagination and developing the awareness of how to bring them into physical form. Everything, everything, everything is already here! There is an abundance, and it has been here since the beginning of time in one form or another.

How can you possibly use your higher faculties if you have no idea or lack knowledge on how to utilize them? Study these amazing instruments of the mind and you'll soon notice how they can assist you in your creative consciousness.

The Six Higher Mental Faculties

"You are to become a creator, not a competitor. You will become a creator by employing the higher faculties with which you have been endowed: Perception, Reason, Will, Memory, Imagination, and Intuition. No other form of life was given these creative faculties."

– Wallace D. Wattles, *The Science of Getting Rich*

1. **Imagination:** While everyone recognizes that they have an imagination, most do not realize the magnificence behind it, much less know how to use it in a constructive way. We think in images, and those images create the environment in our mind. Imagination is a powerful force. It can take you anywhere in the world with just one thought. It can put you under a palm tree in Hawaii, on a yacht soaking up the sun, or even sitting in the driver's seat of your dream car. Look around you. Everything you see began with a thought through someone's imagination. Things are created twice. First in the mind and then in the physical form. We all have a mental tool that is just sitting dormant in our minds until we awaken it with a command. Great ideas come from pure imagination. Build an image in your mind of the kind of life you want to live. The universe is willing to unveil itself to anyone who comes into harmony with how it works. Be determined to think for yourself without any outside influence or interference and design your life with your imagination. See yourself already in possession of whatever it is that you desire and enjoy what it feels like.

2. **Intuition:** Intuition is energy and the gift of natural knowing. It resides in each of us. You know that gut feeling? Yes, that's the one! Go with it! You know you want to, but your outer senses

take over and then you realize you should have gone with your gut feeling, but you didn't. It happens all the time. Well, that is your intuition, and we were never taught to use this gift as a pertinent tool throughout our lives, yet we all possess it. You see, your intuitive mind picks up on a particular occurrence, a vibration that your outer senses have missed, and it speaks to you. You'll feel it through a vibrational energy, either negative or positive. Have you ever met someone and then noticed an uneasy feeling about him or her? Or have you ever heard someone say, "Wow! I've got a good feeling about this"? Well, it's the vibe! They are picking up on good vibrations. How about walking into someone's home? Haven't you felt what type of energy is in the home without anyone even saying a word? Pay close attention the next time you meet someone or walk into an establishment and see if you can pick up on the energetic vibration in the room.

3. **Will:** Will is the ability to give yourself a command and follow through with it no matter what obstacles get in your way. Now, this is not the same will as in willpower. Willpower is more of a forced decision, and although you may feel committed to a decision it will not last very long and will unvaryingly end with a negative result. The will I am talking about comes from a deeper space within you, a creative spark that holds a fixed mental image in the mind. It is a calm, peaceful, and effortless attitude in making a decision and sticking to it with focus and ease. The frequency of your life will change because of your ability to follow through.

4. **Reason:** Reason is the ability to effectively choose our thoughts. Our reasoning factor is the mental tool we use to think. Our reasoning allows us to form thoughts and pull them all together through a vibrational frequency and build an idea. We are bombarded with daily information such as ideas, conversations, arguments, conflict, solicitations, and so forth. Fortunately, you

don't have to entertain all this confusion at one time. You can initiate your reasoning and block out any unwanted chaos. This is especially important to understand because you become what you think about most of the time.

5. **Memory:** Memory is the result of your mental muscles. Have you ever heard someone say they forgot to do something? Now, some do have weaker memories than others, but just like every other muscle in the body, if you want to improve it, you will need to use it. Truth is, we all have a perfect memory; we just haven't exercised it enough. Your mind is full of memories! Haven't you noticed that certain occurrences jolt your memory about a particular time in your life, and you are able to retrieve a memory that was filed away oh so many years ago? It's all there. You have a lifetime full of memories stored away.

6. **Perception:** Perception is what one believes to be true, as beliefs determine one's perception. Depending on how the subject at hand is approached, there can be many points of view on any given subject or circumstance. Past experiences and present feelings all play a huge role in one's perception today. You may see a circumstance as a blessing and another may see it as a curse. Each life experience provides a perspective, and that perspective becomes our perception of life as a whole.

The Gift of Mental Faculties

Have you ever wondered what you are really capable of? Can you imagine what your life would look like if you learned how to use the power of your mind on a conscious level? We have been enriched with the ability to choose how we will live our lives. It is simply up to us to use our imagination to design and create the life we so desire. God has given us the gift of mental faculties so that we may use them for the highest good. Take the time to pursue the knowledge and understanding of how to best use what's already on the inside of you.

Learning how to use your six higher faculties will help you tap into the non-physical side of yourself. When using your higher faculties, you are not dependent on an outside circumstance or condition. You are strictly dealing with the invisible, the deep spiritual essence of who you are. Each of us houses a divine intelligence within that surpasses our human capabilities.

Oh, You Have It!

Since I was a young child I was very aware of my intuition, but unaware there was a name for it. Even as I grew older I didn't think of it as a power of the mind because I always felt it in the gut. I shrugged it off because it frightened me, and I simply didn't understand what was happening through me. I thought if I just ignored it, it would go away. To be so young and have such strong powers of the mind, I was afraid to share my experiences with anyone. It wasn't until my teenage years that I gained enough courage to mention it to my mother.

When I was fifteen I asked my mother, "How come every time I think about something it happens?" She exclaimed, "Oh, you have it!" With a look of concern, I replied, "Have what?" And she said, "One of your great aunts was a witch." It took me years to build up enough courage to finally share my thoughts with her, and I walked away thinking I was a witch. It wasn't her fault. She had no idea about intuition or the power of the mind. I didn't dare tell her about the dreams I had and how each one revealed itself within days, or how every time I looked at the clock it was 11:11 or somehow always seventeen minutes past the hour.

I knew these weren't considered "normal" occurrences for everyone else, but they were certainly normal to me. I just didn't understand why. My mother later explained that back in the old days when someone spoke of their power they were considered a witch. All I knew was that I had some sort of power. Interestingly enough, my son Josh asked me the exact same question when he was just ten years old. You see, I knew I harnessed an amazing power, but I didn't know how or why, and my own mother couldn't even explain it to me. Today I am grateful to know how important a role my higher faculties and especially my intuition have played in my life.

Here's Your Sign

Have you ever felt like the universe was trying to tell you something? We've been taught to think that anything we don't understand is evil or just coincidental. But I believe in messages from the universe, our loved ones, and our spirit guides. I believe they are always conspiring to communicate with us. I'll often be thinking of something and a sign appears right there in front of me. We are all surrounded by signs, but most pay little to no attention to them if they recognize them at all. You must be willing to receive the signs for them to be revealed to you. As your consciousness grows so will the power of your mind. You'll become more in tune and aware of receiving messages.

There is no limit on how the universe will converse with you. You may possibly receive a sign through a billboard, a passing bus, a song on the radio, a TV commercial, or a conversation. Whatever the case may be, just be open and start paying attention to what you are experiencing. Many people speak of seeing red cardinals, butterflies, or even dragonflies, and they believe it to be a sign from their loved ones who have passed on. I've also heard of unexpected electrical activity, a certain fragrance, smelling smoke, or even just sensing someone's presence. More examples could include number sequences such as these: 000, 111, 222, 333, 444, 555, 666, 777, 888, 999, 22, 123, 617, and 1111. Each has its own meaning.

I can't help but think about how often the forces of the universe have dazzled me throughout my lifetime and continue to do so today. Recently I was in a bookstore with a friend, looking for a certain book. While my hands were full I spotted several clerks whizzing by. I pointed to one and asked Kathy to ask her for assistance in finding the book we wanted. When Kathy mentioned the name of the book, the clerk looked down into her very own hands and said, "Oh, here, do you mean this one?" I could see the blood draining right out of Kathy's face as she walked over to me, stunned at what had just happened. I couldn't help but giggle and say, "Welcome to my world." You will notice that when you are in the flow things like this will happen all the time. Dazzled once again, I expressed my gratitude and moved on.

The Power Is in the Thought

"There's a difference between wishing for a thing and being ready to receive it. No one is ready for a thing until he believes he can acquire it. The state of mind must be belief, not mere hope or wish."

– Napoleon Hill, *Think and Grow Rich*

A few years back my son thought it would be resourceful to get his real estate license since he managed over 150 condominiums. Even though he studied fervently, he got spooked and approached the test with the idea that he was not smart enough to pass. Well, he failed. That failure sent him into victim mode. He felt unworthy and was very down on himself. To sum it up, it was a tough blow to his ego. You can make yourself feel as good or bad as you want in any situation. He did a really good job of beating himself up in this one. Life will swallow you whole if you allow it.

He put his dream of receiving his real estate license on the back burner for a few years. In the interim he studied human potential and self-development. He developed the power of his mind and learned how to change his way of thinking. Utilizing the power of the mind through imagination of thought can improve any circumstance. He became a cooperative component to his desire. He shifted the power of his mind from wanting to expecting, and he learned to see the world around him through a new lens with a sharper vision.

Two years later he confidently returned with a conscious effort to retake the test with a better attitude of thought. This time he imagined himself passing. Not only did he go from failing the test and feeling unworthy to retaking the test, finishing early, and feeling exuberant, but he successfully passed it. The only thing he did differently was use the power of his mind. He cast a declarative image in his mind going in expecting to pass. He changed the way he thought about himself and imagined a passing grade.

I think we all have the desire to succeed and become the best version of ourselves, but we get lost in negative self-talk and judging our own capability, or we're too concerned about what other people think. We all have the ability to manage our vibration based on the thoughts we choose. Be willing to let your desires be shown to you. Just like my son, we are all capable of making changes in our lives. We don't always see the beauty in the struggle because while it is stretching us beyond our comfort zone, we focus more on the pain rather than the growth. He could have let this one obstacle in his life stop him from going any further, but he didn't. It may have taken him two years to face the test again, but he did it. He soon learned how much discipline it requires to shift a paradigm. Something significant changed in his thinking, and his awareness level shifted from his typical pattern of thought. There's a huge difference in wishing for a thing and being ready to receive it. This time he was ready to receive it.

Passing the test the second time around meant so much more to him than just receiving his real estate license. For the first time in his life he felt like he overcame adversity and achieved something that he actually believed in. That experience triggered something amazing in him and he hasn't looked back. A person really can achieve what they believe they can achieve through the power of the mind. He had the same potential the first time he went in to take the test as he did the second time. The difference was belief, not mere hope or wish.

Your Inner Counsel

Your inner counsel is present at all times. As you tap into this inner wisdom, you will notice the desires of your heart are just waiting to be expressed. Their only requirement is your willingness to be aware of them. Notice what you are noticing as experiences and opportunities present themselves. You will soon begin to understand that the power of the mind is far greater than any spoken language. As we learn to appreciate the brilliance of the mind, more so than any logical thoughts, these finely tuned senses will help guide each of us through our journey of life. Use them wisely.

Loving Reminders:

- ♥ The wisdom of life is awareness.
- ♥ You cannot change what you are not willing to acknowledge.
- ♥ We have been programmed to become servants to the rational mind.
- ♥ There is a life force behind your creative power.
- ♥ Becoming aware of these extraordinary faculties is the first step in learning how to utilize them.
- ♥ Everything, everything, everything is already here.
- ♥ Learning how to use your mental faculties will help you tap into the non-physical side of yourself.
- ♥ Have you ever wondered what you are really capable of?
- ♥ The activity of the mind is thought, and your thoughts absolutely create your environment.
- ♥ It is simply up to us to use our imagination to design and create the life we so desire.

FOUR

THE PROGRAMMING OF YOUR EGO, CONDITIONING, AND PARADIGMS, OH MY!

There seems to be a wondrous air about life and the variety of experiences and opportunities available to us all once we learn about the universal laws and the power of the mind. By sincerely learning how to align and harmonize with them you will have gained a better understanding of how your choices and actions have influenced the outcome and design of your life. Everything in this world is orchestrated perfectly, and although many people assume life just happens to them with no rhyme or reason, the truth is life happens for them and through them according to how they utilize the universal laws and the power of the mind.

Our thoughts dictate our lives. But do you know why you think the way you do? As you begin to shift into a higher version of yourself, you will meet with obstacles along the way. Many of these obstacles will come in the form of programming. We have all been programmed to think a certain way through our ego, conditioning, and paradigms. Although you cannot see them, they are controlling your life. Before you can move forward and break through these obstacles, it's important to know how and where your programming originated. The greater the understanding, the greater the opportunity for change.

Programming is the biggest reason people do not evolve. Many succumb to what they have been conditioned to believe, and if they even consider changing they inherit a label: the black sheep of the family. How often have you wanted to pursue a certain career or even speak about something that was important to you, but because you feared being shamed by your family and friends you gave in and remained silent? You learned this behavior from someone somewhere during your lifetime. This is why so many dreams are left behind and fade away. This is why so many people are living a lie. Slowly but surely, we suppress our many pieces of authenticity to keep the peace and make others happy.

The Voice of Ego

Our egos have been built through every one of our experiences in life. In chapter one, I referred to the ego by describing a time in my life when I thought that's who I was. Many will also mistakenly identify themselves as their ego. But you see, ego is just an illusion of who you think you are. In other words, who you are and who you think you are, are two totally different things. Who you think you are is just an imaginary viewpoint that you have conjured up in your mind. That's how and why ego interferes with our thinking, causing the human part of us to feel self-conscious, unworthy, discontent, bitter, angry, and depressed. This false identity is rooted in fear and doesn't like transparency. It worries, has regrets, is jealous, inflicts judgment, and is very competitive all because it assumes you live in a world of scarcity. All these traits are indulgences to the egoic mind. Learn to recognize them and identify how the voice of ego is influencing your life.

A few years back I actually thought it would be best if I completely forgot about my ego, Gangsta Wendy, and never mention her again.

But then I realized I would just be shunning a vital part of myself. What I have learned is that I should embrace her and what she stood for. She has been there for me when I felt like no one else was. She is strength, she is weakness, and she is absolutely what I make her out to be. I am not condoning her actions, merely recognizing them, and only now do I have a deeper understanding of them. When our core self does not demonstrate enough strength to face certain circumstances, the ego will dash to the front of any situation and take over. It tricks you into thinking it is protecting you. The key is to be consciously aware of the type of energy that is attached to the ego and projected out into the world. Gangsta Wendy represents a part of my life that taught me many lessons.

My shift in consciousness enabled me to break through the wall of programming. Through that process I felt my burdens being lifted, and I felt lighter and lighter. It was the most beautiful feeling in the world, like when you see light at the end of a tunnel. I felt empowered. My excitement for life grew stronger and stronger. Peace, love, gratitude, joy, and forgiveness emerged. My higher-self was finally able to see beyond other people's expectations, diminishing the all-pervading voice of ego. I have learned that when you are guided inwardly you are acting in accordance with your true nature, your authentic self, and this allows you to connect deeply with Spirit.

Vroom! Vroom!

In the past my ego went into overdrive when I dwelled on thoughts of anger, fear, and frustration and especially when a person didn't quite understand how a four-way stop worked. Responding to the loud dictation of my ego, Gangsta Wendy often made it a point to explain to the offender how a four-way stop worked.

On another occasion, while driving along the coast, someone was driving in front of me and as they switched lanes rocks flew up onto the front of my new corvette. Vroom! Vroom! I was so angry! What if he scratched my car? My emotions took over, and I vigorously chased the poor guy down with my husband in tow in the passenger seat. As we approached a red light, I pulled right up next to him and rolled my husband's window down. If you can picture this, my husband slid down in his seat just as his window went down. I started yelling at that poor guy over a few rocks, and he ended up taking off through the red light. My heart was beating so fast, and just as I witnessed my ego high-fiving itself, my husband yelled, "That guy could have shot you!" I looked at him and said, "And I would have caught that bullet!" I reached up into thin air, as if to catch the bullet. I can assure you he was not amused, and although I am not proud of moments like this, my ego was beaming and felt quite justified.

Throughout the years, and even more so recently, I began to see my behavior in other people and something just clicked. I secretly imagined the angels saying, "Hallelujah, it's about time!" I remember thinking, *Wow! Is that what I look like when I get angry?* The Law of Reflection can be very humbling. Once I became consciously aware of my behavior, I knew I had to put myself in check. Ego is in it to win it and has its sights set on long-term survival. I have always reacted when I felt confronted, and to be anything different wouldn't be me, or so I thought. I was conditioned to speak my piece or prove my point.

The unavoidable truth here is that I was clearly living in an egoic hypnotic state. I was reactive and didn't even know why. It wasn't until I removed my wall that I began to understand that my reactive state was never ever about what the other person did or said. It was about me and all the built-up burdens I had stored deep down inside of me. Mentally releasing these stored up egoic thoughts of fear and frustration has allowed a flow of greater good to enter into my life. This is why we should all cast our burdens.

Because I experienced a shift in consciousness, it has helped me understand my actions. When you alter the paradigm, you alter your life. Thankfully I am such a different person today and I practice a peaceful mindset. I am happy to share that I don't feel the need to give anyone a crash course in driver's ed any longer. I *choose* to take the high road and I don't look back. I focus on remaining calm and have learned to let go of the negative way of doing things, and this has led me to consciously connect with my heart.

It Starts Early

We are born into a world where we are *told* who we are instead of being allowed to navigate through life and *discover* who we are without the judgment of others. Since conception, we have absorbed the outer environment of our surroundings, which started our conditioning. We were raised in an environment where we ate the same foods as our family did, we followed the same religion as our parents, and even spoke the same language. Children who have been adopted from all over the world are brought into new homes and adapt to their new parents' conditioning.

Because the conditioned mind runs on autopilot, we do and say things without even thinking. Can you think of a time when someone asked you a question and you just blurted out an answer without even knowing why you have a certain belief about the answer you provided? It used to happen to me all the time. My programming conveniently kicked in! This is what I mean when I say *we don't even know who we are.*

As a society we have become sheeple, conforming to what we have been exposed to. Most have not looked beyond or, worse yet, even looked within to understand what it is they truly believe in or not. Over the years, we've all experienced layers upon layers of ego, conditioning, and paradigms. Our environment has placed upon us everything from media to music, movies, clothing, education, brand of automobile, political views, views about money, and so forth. It isn't until we meet someone with different views that we take inventory of our own thoughts and notice the labels we have subconsciously inherited.

The Power of Suggestion Is Real

In my early twenties, I went to visit my mother in Atlanta. While we were making sandwiches, my sister yelled out, "No mayo on mine!" I personally love mayonnaise, so I said, "I didn't realize you didn't like mayonnaise." And she said, "I've never liked mayonnaise." My mother laughed as she interjected, "She doesn't like mayonnaise because her grandmother doesn't like mayonnaise, and her grandmother has *told her* that she doesn't like mayonnaise." My sister just shrugged her shoulders and gave me a look of confusion, as she had no real explanation for herself. That is a simple yet obvious example of conditioning.

Ever since she was a child she had been conditioned to think she didn't like mayonnaise. My sister wouldn't even try it because she was afraid to go against her own conditioned beliefs. Think about how you have been programmed through your conditioning throughout your entire life. It was only by accident years later that her husband, Matt, added mayonnaise to a sandwich he was making for her. In that first bite, my sister discovered just how much she actually liked mayonnaise.

The power of suggestion is real. Ever have someone plant a deliberate idea in your mind about how their encounter went with another person, place, or thing only to have your experience play out the exact same way? Most of us are programmed to go in looking for the suggested outcome. We are surrounded by a myriad of influences. For example, just look at the TV. It tells us what to eat, what to wear, and what to believe in. The television programs are certainly doing their job. There's also radio, social media, human beings as stated above, and so much more that offers a suggestive outcome.

Now, let me assure you there's a positive side to all of this too. The power of suggestion can also be used as a tool to help get you through a rough time or just through a normal day by waking up and saying, "Today is going to be a great day!" It could possibly assist you in passing a test, winning a game, or even meeting the love of your life simply by suggesting and believing it is so. You have the power within, so use it wisely. Listen to the words you are using to shape your life.

The False Self

As a result of conditioning, most people hide behind their own wall of insecurities or some sort of mask to fit in between the fine lines of what is socially accepted and what has been expected of them throughout their entire lives. This type of conditioning creates the false self. Sadly, many get so used to living this way that they completely forget who they really are. I certainly was no exception. It wasn't until I surrendered into the shift that I shed that miserable wall and began to live an authentic life.

Look around; the conditioned mind will keep many stuck in loveless marriages, unfulfilling friendships, unrewarding jobs, and simply living a life that does not give them life. This is heartbreaking. We are too wrapped up in what we think other people will think, so we settle for a life of regrets. Your incessant mind chatter will continue to beat you down to make sure you remain in your comfort zone doing exactly what you have been programmed and conditioned to do.

Living a life of false appearances will leave a hole in you. Feeling empty, you continue to live a lie, portraying a life that is really non-existent. You see, when you're living a life that is not in alignment with your truth, everything thereafter begins to unravel. It may seem so insignificant at the time, and you may not even notice, but as time goes on you start to wonder, *Will things ever go my way?* Feelings such as anger, resentment, depression, and anxiousness will rise to the surface.

Oftentimes, after repeatedly giving your time, energy, and money toward a life that you're not in alignment with, it will leave you feeling completely depleted. That's not living. That's existing. It isn't until you become fully conscious, aware, and present in your life that you will begin to initiate the desired change and make a necessary shift. Most people are unaware that they've been programmed and have accepted everything they've been exposed to. Their beliefs have been embedded deep within the subconscious mind, and that's exactly where ego, conditioning, and paradigms reside.

A Group of Ideas, a Collection of Beliefs, and a Multitude of Habits

The truth is, the mind has been absorbing repetitive language for years. We have been programmed both genetically and environmentally. Our paradigms, being a group of ideas, a collection of beliefs, and a multitude of habits, have been passed down to us from prior generations. They have been instilled in us and have shaped our lives through listening to the views of our parents, grandparents, peers, teachers, and so forth. As a child your subconscious mind was like that of a sponge. It absorbed whatever happened around you. These thoughts took root and grew with you as you grew older. The mind continues to collect and reserve gained information, thus playing a huge role in your perception. This is how we've developed our worldview.

Not only do paradigms control our perception, but they control our creativity, work habits, the foods we eat, the way we think about money, and the way we utilize our time, just to name a few. To sum it up, paradigms have complete control over your life and don't allow much room for growth. Your internal programs are controlling your every move. If you want to change your results, you must be willing to interrupt your programming. As we all know, this is not always an easy thing to do. For a paradigm shift to occur there must be significant change in the way one thinks or perceives something. Then and only then will the old paradigm be replaced by a new way of thinking.

Growing up, I was exposed to certain beliefs about money, religion, and education. My friends who grew up in other countries followed the same belief system as their families. But when you are exposed to new information you may begin to question what you have been led to believe your entire life.

Many people have paradigms about money. I remember when my husband turned fifty years old. He has wanted a 51-foot catamaran for as long as I can remember. Even though he is a successful businessman, he had a money paradigm that went something like this: *Since I didn't achieve my dream of buying a million-dollar yacht by the time I turned fifty years old, then what in the world makes me think I will be able to buy one in the next twenty years or so?*

Just three years later he was introduced to a new way of thinking, and two years after that he purchased his million-dollar yacht. He changed his paradigm about money. He focused on making every single day a successful day, and over time he replaced the old paradigm with a brand new one. One that served him well. We are habitual creatures. You first have to recognize the habit (paradigm) that is not serving you before you can replace it with a new habit (paradigm) that will.

I truly believe that most people do want more out of life. A part of them wants to move forward, but a bigger part of them continues to remain stuck in the paradigm, and they don't know how to break through it. This mental programming stops them in their tracks every time. The paradigm controls the behavior, not the intellect. The good news is that you can definitely overcome your paradigms, but it will take a lot of work. You have to remember that you have been programmed since conception to think a certain way, behave a certain way, and believe in certain things. That was the learning part; now you will have to unlearn those habits and learn new ones. Ones that will support you in reaching your highest potential.

The only way to make a paradigm shift is through constant spaced repetition or by experiencing an emotional impact. The sobering reality is that most people will begin their day by habit and end their day by the same habits. Nothing new will have changed. They will follow the same routine as the day before, and the paradigm will continue to pull them back into the comfort zone even if they try something new. Eventually they will make excuses and justify the life they are living, which will only illuminate their comfort zone. I bid you to look at your current results. If you truly want a different result, you must be willing to change your paradigm.

Heaven on Earth

There will come a time when you begin to peel back the layers of your life and take notice of what you are truly aligned with. This is your truth. It is so empowering to have control over your own thoughts. Remember, this is a learned practice. It's part of unlearning and relearning. If you can just delete, delete, delete what you have learned and focus intently on relearning, you'll be pleasantly surprised as you approach life with a whole new perspective. It could very well be the key to opening heaven right here on earth for you. I know it has been for me. I certainly had a lot of unlearning and relearning to do myself.

It's not going to happen overnight, so don't get frustrated. Don't plan for the demise of your unhealthy ego, conditioning, or even your paradigms, but rather set them up for love. Yes, love for all the false beliefs you were introduced to. Love for the part of you that thrived on drama and external validation because you didn't feel whole. Love for the part of you that was unkind because love is essentially who you are. Don't continue to beat yourself up because you were involved in negativity or raised a certain way. Once you have identified how the compelling forces of your programming have affected your life, you are more likely to be successful in shutting down their power over you.

A shift in your fixed mental patterns must happen if you wish to change or improve upon your life. By consistently impressing upon the subconscious mind a new way to think, you are creating new neural pathways toward change. Because you've been hardwired to think a certain way for so long, you are bound to experience resistance from your old way of thinking. These changes may not even be notice- ably different at first; just know that internally the old conditioning will eventually fade away and will become weaker as you gain strength in a new way to think. One day you will awaken to a whole new world with the renewal of your mind.

Loving Reminders:

- ♥ Our thoughts dictate our lives.
- ♥ Ego is just an illusion of who you think you are.
- ♥ Cast your burdens.
- ♥ When you alter the paradigm, you alter your life.
- ♥ The conditioned mind runs on autopilot.
- ♥ Our minds have been absorbing repetitive language for years.
- ♥ The paradigm controls the behavior, not the intellect.
- ♥ Learn, unlearn, and relearn

FIVE

CREATING POSITIVE CHANGE
THROUGH YOUR ACTIONS, THOUGHTS,
AND WORDS

Resistance to change manifests itself in many ways through the rooted beliefs of one's ego, conditioning, and paradigms. Expansion of self requires change, and although many want change, they aren't willing to change themselves. While it's easy to find fault in others, we conveniently overlook the necessary changes that need to occur in our own lives. To regain control of your life, it is essential to create positive changes through your actions, thoughts, and words. Many run from themselves. They deflect and avoid necessary conversations about the flow or trajectory of their own lives. When you resist change, you resist growth. Change is good. It offers new experiences and exposure to new opportunities.

Your personal growth greatly depends on new challenges. Creating positive change is more than just slapping a smile on your face and force-feeding *positivity*. It has to come from within. It is a learned practice. As you brave new pathways, everything on the inside will begin to shift, and as you move forward you will leave a trail of influence, inspiring others to do the same.

Coachable, Teachable, and Trainable

Without question, living up to your potential requires the expansion of self. You achieve this by consistently learning something new. In order to create positive change in your life, consider this question: Are you coachable, teachable, and trainable? Let's break down these important skills:

Being coachable requires listening with the intention of learning something new. There is infinite wisdom in being coachable, but in the case of the know-it-all, they barely listen while waiting to share what they already know. *This isn't my first rodeo* is a common response. Before you can finish a sentence, they express their thoughts without any regard for your efforts. In order to be teachable, one must be willing to approach each day as a new opportunity to learn, grow, and expand. A key component to being teachable is the ability to accept feedback from others without being defensive. This isn't always an easy thing to do, but as one advances in awareness feedback is invited. To be trainable is to ensure that you are eager to improve in many or all areas of life.

Many inherently think they possess these traits and say they are ready to do whatever it takes to transform their lives. But all too often they aren't willing to do the necessary work. If you truly want to create positive change through your actions, thoughts, and words, be willing to read a new book, one that will influence you in ways that encourage growth. Step out of your comfort zone. Attend a seminar both near and far. Make new friends. Join a mastermind group and be open to suggestions, feedback, and change.

You can measure the cost of all these suggestions. Some may cost you time and money while others may cost you your ego. But the real truth is you will never be able to measure what you gain from them. Your decision to do none, some, or even all of these suggestions will denote whether you are coachable, teachable, and trainable. Decide to make an investment in yourself for yourself. Be willing to be in service of the life that is seeking to emerge through you.

One Step at a Time

Whether you are satisfied with where you are in life or not, your current results did not happen overnight. You got here one step at a time and one decision at a time. You will achieve positive changes through incorporating one small step at a time as long as you remain consistent in your efforts. This remains true for regaining a healthier lifestyle in the form of mind, body, and spirit. It also remains true for your financial situation, changing the way you think, decluttering your life, serving others, and anything else you can possibly think of. As the saying goes, "A journey of a thousand miles begins with a single step." If you try to approach any change by contemplating the vastness of it all at once, you will automatically feel resistance. It is the small consistent steps that will significantly invoke everlasting change.

Most people are resistant to change, and big radical changes immediately trigger fear and interrupt our thinking. We shut down and lose sight of all creativity. We've been wired to resist change and to resist being changed. Because of this, the best way to incorporate change is through one small step at a time. This one simple suggestion can and will make a huge impact on the results in your life. The process of change begins with the awareness of your desire. As you identify what it is that you truly want to change, hold the vision of the end result. When you begin to take action, you will notice the positive effects it has on your life right away.

Don't wait until you have achieved your desired change to celebrate. Celebrate along the way. Every small step toward your goal is a tiny victory that should be celebrated. That alone will boost your drive and enthusiasm as you continue to move forward. Embrace it, celebrate it, and love yourself through it all. Change does not happen overnight. Continue, stick with it, and before you know it many changes will be underway. Be patient and willing to open yourself up to life's most rewarding and fulfilling experiences.

Release the Negativity

Once you see how your life has been shaped by the world in which you live through your actions, thoughts, and words, you will begin to understand your life story. Your limiting beliefs didn't create themselves, and listening to your internal dialogue only enhances your self-limiting belief patterns.

Although change is not easy, it is necessary for the expansion of growth. How can you expect to live a joyous, purposeful, happy life if you live in a negative mindset or are surrounded by outer sources of negativity? It's bound to take you on a downward spiral. There's no need to live at the mercy of your negative thoughts. If you want to create positive changes and develop a new vision for your life, release the negativity and embrace the following suggestions:

- **Express gratitude:** Expressing gratitude changes your vibration and will put you in a better frame of mind even for the simplest of pleasures.

- **Serve others:** Serving others counters negative feelings and has a positive effect on the body. It nourishes both the giver and receiver.

- **Watch your associations:** Surround yourself with like-minded people who support you, encourage you, and exude positive change.

- **Practice forgiveness:** Forgiveness allows the release of built-up negative energy. It sets you free of the burden and allows you to move into a more positive way of being.

- **Be kind:** "The Golden Rule" says to treat others the way you would like to be treated. Be kind and meaningful in your interactions with others. We also rise by lifting others.

- **Take accountability for yourself:** No more playing the role of victim. You are now consciously in control of holding yourself accountable for what you have created in your life.

We have all experienced disruptive challenges, but as you embrace these suggestions you will feel less challenged and more heart centered. You need not worry about those who ridicule your efforts. When you are anchored in the heart, you become receptive to higher influences, and negativity begins to dissipate. It is all an attitude of the mind. Let this be a turning point in your life toward creating positive change through your actions, thoughts, and words.

Responding vs. Reacting

Responding versus reacting will influence your life in ways that create positive change. Reacting oftentimes reveals underlying assumptions, fears, and insecurities with a more aggressive approach. When emotions take over, rage causes unproductive arguments. This defense mechanism usually backfires, leaving many feeling regretful of the things they have said or done in the heat of the moment. Even someone you least expect can lose their composure at times. If you don't allow yourself to process your emotions, they will at some point be expressed in a more damaging way. Irrational behavior doesn't solve anything. Can you think of a time when you reacted to something that didn't warrant your reaction? I sure can. Chaos only adds more chaos. As you begin to define your awareness, you will be better able to detect the root cause of your outbursts.

When you get upset, as hard as it may be to believe, you are choosing to be upset. So simple, yet so misunderstood. People, events, or circumstances cannot make you get upset unless you allow it. This was a *huge* revelation for me, and one that you certainly owe to yourself. It is then and only then that you will be able to understand the recurring themes in your life. Fine tune your thinking and focus on the betterment of creating positive changes in your life by responding rather than reacting. Responding contains reasoning, thus allowing a conscious decision to come from a place of integrity. You are the only one who has total control over your actions, thoughts, and words.

Without fail, daily life will spring unexpected circumstances, but how you react/respond says a lot. There is always a root cause. How do you act during heavy traffic situations? Or better yet, how do you act with your spouse or partner during a heated discussion? What about work, family situations, or even the children? Direct your awareness to the deeper issues embedded within and be brave enough to ask yourself, *Why am I so upset? Why did this bother me so much? Did I really scream at my children because they made a little mess when I'm really annoyed because I had a bad day at the office?* That reaction is the remnants of blocked energy. We all have the right to react or respond. Just understand that you are responsible for the way you feel about something, so don't take it out on innocent bystanders.

I have many stories about how Gangsta Wendy used to react versus respond and how it didn't serve me well. Fortunately, changing the way I think has created positive changes in my life and alleviated much agony. This proved especially true while traveling with my husband on one particular trip. Our suitcases did not make it to our connecting flight. We landed in the middle of the night and planned to be at a 9 a.m. seminar the next day. We had toiletries, but I was missing makeup, hair supplies, and my favorite shoes and clothing, and my husband was missing his favorites as well.

We were notified that it would be twenty-four hours before we received our luggage. As soon as we made it to our hotel, we kissed goodnight and my husband said, "I know you have changed because normally you'd be pitching a fit over this!" As if he were waiting for me to explode. I just looked at him and smiled. I hadn't even noticed my behavior until he mentioned it. I remember feeling very proud of myself in the observance of my newfound perspective on life. We woke up and attended the seminar wearing the same clothes and makeup from the day before.

Although this was a successful paradigm shift in myself, it takes time to develop this sort of response. Once you do, it just becomes a natural state of being. I didn't revert to my old way of thinking because I learned how to process my thoughts by reconditioning my mind. Why give energy toward uncontrollable situations? Getting upset and acting out would not have helped our situation. In fact, it would have made it worse. By responding instead of reacting, I remained in a good vibration and it felt wonderful.

Expression of Thought

"By thy words thou shalt be justified
and by thy words thou shalt be condemned."
Matthew 12:37

What you say to yourself matters on many levels. Every thought going on inside of you is an expression of itself on the outside of you. You hide nothing. When you come up with a thought about yourself, either negative or positive, your conscious mind has the power to either accept it or reject it. Once accepted, that thought sinks directly into the subconscious mind, and that's when you will begin to see the expression of it on the outside. That expression of thought may show up as happiness, sadness, self-doubt, sickness, health, confidence, low self-esteem, or just about anything you can think of. By creating positive changes through your actions, thoughts, and words, you will slowly recondition your subconscious mind.

Have you ever noticed how the folks who always complain about being sick seem to always be sick? Or how about the ones who say, "I'll never get a break!" And they always seem to have a black cloud hovering over their heads. I actually overheard someone say that he just wanted to earn enough money to pay off his student loans. Do you see the self-sabotage here in the expression of thought? Then there's the living-in-lack scenario: *We don't have the money to buy this* or *I'll never be able to afford that.* One of the biggest complaints I often overhear is: *What else could go wrong today?* Well, the laws will not disappoint! Asking that question is like opening Pandora's box! You will get *exactly* what you are focusing on. These types of thoughts project negativity, causing self-victimization. You will not achieve prosperity if your energetic frequency is that of lack. The words you speak so freely today are governing your life tomorrow.

When you open yourself up to negative influences such as these, you are doing none other than self-sabotage. Ever spend the day or even just a few hours with someone who complains about *everything*? Or worse yet, the same thing over and over? Geeze, it's exhausting to listen to it. They have become so accustomed to that dominant vibration that they are practically oblivious to what they are sharing. It seems perfectly normal to them. Every circumstance in their life is an ordeal. Something is always wrong or never goes their way. It's their vibration. They are operating from a negative frequency. You get back what you put out. To create positive changes in their life, they will need to change the frequency they are on, just like a song on the radio. If you don't like that song, you change the station to a new frequency, one with a song you do like. It's that easy. Be mindful of the dominant vibrational frequency you are on and what you are spewing out into the universe.

Here is an example of how to create positive change in the words you speak. My assistant, Amanda, once said to me, "I don't want to disappoint you." I asked her to rephrase what she just said but in a more positive way. She came up with, "I want to make you proud." Do you see the difference?

In essence, both statements have the same meaning. Even though she meant it in a positive way, her first statement ended negatively. The second statement ended in a positive way. Had she continued to think and feel that she didn't want to disappoint me, she would have remained in a negative vibration filled with fear of making mistakes. But by changing her words she began to smile as she spoke them aloud. Her body language was even noticeably different, for the better. While she was using negative words and phrases, thinking that she was being positive and supportive, she was actually sending out negative energy. Amanda was speaking the words, but she was not listening to the words that were coming out of her mouth. When we change our thoughts, we change our lives forever.

Think Before You Post

Our mind is like an ocean of never-ending thoughts. In today's society, those thoughts are instantly shared on social media. Although social media can be fun, entertaining, and a great way to keep in touch with family and friends, it is a breeding ground for negativity. Many people use it to vent about people, places, and things. One can end up being a victim of identity theft or even experience cyberbullying. Most don't think of the future consequences that may arise from previous posts. We run the risk of losing a job, a friendship, or even a personal relationship when we post things out of context. Ask yourself, is this really how I want to show up in the world?

We've become the victims of other people's negativity. Not only are we carrying around our own suppressed negative energy, we are also subconsciously absorbing others'. We all know that one person who constantly thrives on posting about their drama. We unknowingly inherit that vibration. That negative energy pours directly into our subconscious mind like a waterfall. It's like a bad infection that keeps spreading across the world. No wonder we feel so weighed down with all this negativity polluting our mental environment. When you're in the presence of negativity or catch yourself reading negative information, create positive change by asking yourself: *Do I really need to know about this?* Either walk away, keep scrolling, or better yet, hit delete and save yourself from unnecessary negativity.

Positive change begins with you. Hold yourself accountable for your actions on social media. We are socially connected and interconnected with millions of people at any given moment. Social media allows us to have an interactive online audience at our fingertips 24/7. How you choose to show up and use this technology is up to you, but there will be consequences. Consciously choosing to share positive thoughts will generate a positive flow of energy. This is where the focus should be. You can actually feel the energy in the statements, whether negative or positive, and they often spawn a long list of contributing responses, only intensifying the original energy. Be aware of everything that presents itself to your mind, and think before you post.

Be Your Own Gatekeeper

You are responsible for who and what you let in and out of your life. By being your own gatekeeper, you'll create positive change by distancing yourself from negative influences. A wise gatekeeper knows when to open the gate and when to close it. The people you surround yourself with have a huge impact on your life. While some may enrich your life, others may suck the life right out of you. Take notice of the people who are happy for your happiness and who support your current journey. They are your vibe tribe. Your vibe tribe will love you through it all. They will support you, encourage you, celebrate you, be truthful, allow for mistakes, forgive you, and catch you when you fall.

Examine your current relationships and see if they meet with these requirements. You will know your vibe tribe when you meet them. In fact, they will be attracted to you because your energetic vibration will be one and the same. It will feel easy and comfortable, definitely not forced. This also gives you an opportunity to be just as supportive of them.

Affirming Your Power

We create the world we live in by the dominant thoughts we allow in our minds. These thought forces, whether good or bad, shape our lives. I just think that is fascinating! We have been designed with the capability of imaginative thought, and the power is in the thought.

A great way to create positive change in your life is by implementing daily affirmations. Each of us houses different desires of the heart, so your affirmations will be unique to you. The way you experience life greatly depends on your thinking. Many miss out on all the wonderful opportunities that life has to offer simply because they don't expect them or they don't believe they are worthy of receiving them. One way to change this is by affirming your power.

Creating positive change will improve the way you perceive yourself and will make a huge impact on your life. Affirming your power begins by making a concentrated effort to change the way you think in a way that better serves you. By creating positive paradigms, relearning how to think, and coming from a place of belief, our lives will begin to unfold just as we have imagined. Visualization is key. This is where your higher faculties come into play by using your imagination of thought and having the will to hold your vision. It's a matter of reprogramming your subconscious mind.

The DeMaren family has three boys. Monica DeMaren shares how she and her husband, Chris, were able to get their children involved in affirming their power by using a mirror exercise.

"My boys have witnessed my husband and me talking to ourselves in the mirror for years. They have also witnessed and experienced the positive changes in our lives over the years too. So when we suggested that they start saying their own affirmations, they were really excited to participate. We started off by asking them to think about what they didn't like because by being aware of this first it made it easier for them to think of the opposite and write it out.

Each child is so different and has their own individual affirmations. They are short and to the point. They keep them taped to the bathroom mirror so that every morning and every evening after brushing their teeth they are reminded to look in the mirror and say their words. They have been working on different affirmations over the last two years and have seen progress in all the areas they wanted to improve on. Our kids are big dreamers too, and they also have affirmations on what their life looks like and feels like when they get older. It's been a lot of fun listening to them dream out loud."

I love how the entire family is involved in dreaming and improving their lives together. Implementing affirmations is a great way to take possession of the mind. Keep them short and sweet and on a positive note from beginning to end. As you work on your affirmations, focus on impressing upon your subconscious mind the desirable feeling of gratitude as if the desire has already been fulfilled. In other words, think about how you will feel when your dream comes true. Excitement, gratitude, and joy, right? Well, stay in that vibration while you are expressing your affirmations and goals.

Don't get discouraged if your desires don't happen overnight. In fact, you may even hear a little voice in your head that goes against everything you affirm. This is normal because you have yet to recondition your subconscious mind. This exercise requires repetition. It will take repetition in all the unlearning and relearning processes. Over time you will instill self-confidence and belief in yourself.

From Struggle to Flow

As you create positive changes through your actions, thoughts, and words, you will begin to notice that your life shifts from struggle to flow, only deepening your life experiences. Creating positive changes will have a lasting effect on your life and may serve as inspiration in the direction of your life goals, financial goals, and spiritual goals. As you shift your thinking toward empowering thoughts and strategies, many opportunities will arise that support your desires. Take notice of the little synchronicities in your life as the universe begins to respond to your thoughts, actions, and words. Lovingly express your gratitude as this occurs. Continue to nurture your life by creating the necessary positive changes, as they will surely impact your life and those around you.

Loving Reminders:

♥ Living up to your potential requires the expansion of self.

♥ "A journey of a thousand miles begins with a single step."

♥ There's no need to live at the mercy of your negative thoughts.

♥ It is all an attitude of the mind.

♥ People, events, or circumstances cannot make you upset unless you allow it.

♥ The words you speak today govern your life tomorrow.

♥ When we change our thoughts, we change our lives forever.

♥ Positive change begins with you.

♥ Find your vibe tribe.

♥ We create the world we live in by the dominant thoughts we allow in our minds.

♥ The way you experience life will greatly depend on your thinking.

♥ Implementing affirmations is a great way to take possession of your mind.

SIX

INTENTIONAL LIVING

Now that you are creating positive changes in your life through your actions, thoughts, and words, it's time to anchor yourself in intentional living. Intentional living allows you to protect your energy, and it offers freedom to do what is most important to you. As you take ownership of your life, you will tend to shift in a new direction and step away from anything that is not in alignment with who you are. You may even start eliminating the non-essential things of less importance and take a step back to evaluate the flow of your life. When you begin to live intentionally, you set the standard for the life you want to live. You and only you know what truly speaks to your heart.

Core Values

Core values are the foundation for intentional living. They will guide you and help you in making daily decisions. In fact, decision making actually becomes very easy once you have established your core values. Remember, we are specifically talking about your core values alone. All too often people will adapt to another's core values and somehow lose sight of what's really important to them. Early on, not everyone will have a good solid idea about what matters most to them, and as time goes on your core values may change. Certain core values may resonate with you more than others, and the really important ones will always remain as top priority in your life.

We all have a moral compass, and when I was in my forties my moral compass began to speak to me loud and clear. When you don't align with your values, you don't feel authentic. I knew I was off course and out of alignment in many aspects of my life. My heartbreaking discontentment was a huge wakeup call for me. It wasn't until I evaluated the flow of my life and understood the absence of some of my very own core values that I formed a clear picture of exactly what I wanted my life to intentionally represent.

So why is it so important to know what your core values are? Well, before you start to live an intentional life, you must have a clear vision of what you will and will not accept in your life. Your vision should embody your core values. Let's say one of your core values is honesty, and your coworker asked you to lie for them. If you are living in your authentic truth, your core value will pop up like a neon sign right in front of your eyes. What will you do? More than likely you will not lie for them. If you do, you will feel resistance in every cell of your body. I'm sure we can all relate to doing something that we didn't really want to do and how it made us feel.

Although your personal core values are unique to you, they will help you establish close relationships with others who either consciously or unconsciously share the same core values. Here are a few examples.

Add to the list as you feel necessary.

Love	Genuine	Integrity
Honesty	Balance	Fitness
Compassion	Positivity	Courage
Reliability	Respect	Trustworthy
Loyalty	Independent	Patience
Commitment	Sober	Open-minded
Family	Wellness	Generous
Helpful	Empowering	Friendship
Humble	Meaning	Philanthropy

These fundamental principles dictate one's behavior. Because we think in images, when someone thinks about you, what list of core values do you think would also appear in their image of you? Try this exercise for yourself. Picture someone in your mind. Now, what core values appear around their image in your mind?

Examine the Flow of Your Life

Many find themselves drifting through life with no real reason or direction behind what they are doing. Examine the flow of your life and ask yourself, *Why am I doing what I'm doing?* Are you merely following a pattern of life, just passing the time, or are your answers backed with intent? Here are a few categories to consider when examining the different areas of your life:

- **Spouse/partner:** Does the vision you have of your relationship match the feeling you carry in your heart? Are you spending time co-creating with the one you love, or do you feel like you are settling for this relationship?

- **Family time:** Do you make time for your family? Are you present and engaged in their lives? How your family interacts with one another will have a great influence over their lives.

- **Career choice:** Is your career choice one of a family tradition that you felt obligated to carry on, or is it one of your own choice? You are likely to spend more time at the office than you will at home. Make sure your career choice is one that is in line with your core values.

- **Health:** Do your habits reflect a healthy lifestyle? The way to transform your health is by transforming your inner dialogue. There will come a time when we will have to ask ourselves if the unhealthy lifestyle was worth it. Your intentions will help you make better choices and will aid in controlling the healthy choices you desire.

- **Money:** Do you have a money consciousness? Do you expand or contract when people talk about money? Many have a general sense of panic when it comes to money. Do you spend money frivolously, or is your spending backed with intention? Have you made wise investments? Are you enabling others with your money? What's your story about money?

- **Friendships:** Your circle of friends have a direct influence on your life. Surround yourself with people who share the same passion and enthusiasm for life as you do. As difficult as it may be, you must separate yourself from negative influencers. Are your friends supportive of your dreams? Do you feel deflated or inspired when you are in their presence? Be selective of who you spend your time with and who you share your ideas with.

- **Personal time:** Although it may feel like a luxury to pamper yourself, it is absolutely necessary. You need time to recharge your mind, body, and spirit. Personal time is different for everyone; just make sure you are allowing yourself the time you need to rejuvenate yourself properly.

- **Clutter:** Do you own your things, or do your things own you? It is time to blow the whistle and start decluttering your life in all areas. I don't think anyone intentionally wants to live in clutter in the physical or non-physical form. When you declutter your life, you declutter your mind and vice versa.

If you are not fulfilled in any one of these categories, maybe it's time to reevaluate the flow of your life and adjust accordingly. When you are lost in negative patterns, they obstruct your ability to live a fulfilled life. Calm your mind and bring yourself to a reflective state. As you gain a deeper understanding of just how much influence your environment has over your life, and how you've become a product of your environment, you will be more apt to make the necessary positive changes. Intentional living is doing what matters most to you. As you evaluate the flow of your life, does it reflect what matters most to you?

Stop and Smell the Roses

Within the last few years, my husband and I have had the most intriguing and meaningful conversations about life, love, family, friends, health, dreams, and goals. It wasn't always like that. For years on end we were on autopilot where intentional living was absent, and one or both of us were always stressed out, enslaved by daily trivia, rushing out the door for work, or you name it. Although I embraced the feeling of accomplishment quite often, I just didn't feel like I was living up to my potential. My sense of fulfillment was null and void. Perhaps you have felt the same way? I know I'm not alone on this journey and there are plenty of people out there just like me searching for more.

When we were together, it seemed like all we ever talked about were dinner choices, weekend plans, or recapping our day at the office. There didn't seem to be any real depth to our conversations. I'm sure there were fleeting moments where we both enjoyed deep conversations over the course of the last twenty-two years; I just knew something inside of me was craving more. I have learned that the more unconscious we are, the more we continue to follow the same well-worn path day in and day out and somehow *still* expect change, but we will never experience change if we aren't willing to change ourselves.

Together, we recently made a unanimous decision that we would stop and smell the roses and live intentionally. We wanted to delve deeper into our lives, explore more, and get to the heart of who we really are. The thought of just waking up, rushing out the door, and throwing ourselves out into the world no longer appealed to us. It felt like we were pulled in every direction once we stepped outside, and the days seemed to be slipping away, leaving only the remnants of a blur. Sure, I get it! It's called life, but it doesn't *have* to be that way.

We added richness to our lives by creating our own reality, so to speak, intentionally living on our terms. We made a conscious decision to take an interest in enjoying life to its fullest. Life in the deepest, sincerest, and most grateful way. We learned that attitude is everything and we have a choice in how we think. Truly understanding this only reinforced our thoughts to flow in a positive direction. Ask anyone how life is treating them. If they give you a negative response, they have a poor attitude toward life. If they give you a positive response, they have a rich attitude toward life.

Oceanfront View

During a trip to Los Angeles, we were enjoying the view of the ocean from a park on Santa Monica Boulevard. We earned a well-deserved break after taking a long brisk walk to and from the Santa Monica Pier. While relaxing on a tattered bench, I took a deep breath and inhaled the crisp ocean breeze. While exhaling gratitude for my beautiful surroundings, I thought to myself, *Wow! I sure could get used to this.*

There was a slight chill in the air and the sun was shining, making it a glorious day. People were riding bikes, exercising, reading books, and walking their dogs. It looked just like a scene from a movie. Right before our eyes we witnessed a jogger pause to stop and smell the roses on a nearby rosebush. My husband and I looked at each other with huge grins. The fact that we witnessed the jogger actually stop and smell the roses was very sweet and sincere in itself, but it harbored an even more profound meaning for both of us.

We were proud of the fact that we were living our lives with intention and in a way that absolutely had more meaning to us. We also knew that seeing the jogger stop and smell the roses was a divine synchronicity. It was supposed to happen, and we were supposed to see it. We believed it was a sign that we were on the right track. We would have missed it had she passed by just five minutes sooner. This led to a discussion about how intentional living was the best thing we could have done for ourselves. It enabled us to evaluate the flow of our lives. It offered us depth and meaning, qualities for which we should all search. We grew bored of the same old, same old as it was no longer satisfying to us, and we felt the need to remove ourselves from the routine that we were so fixated on. We wanted to thrive and continue to grow as individuals, as a couple, and as a family.

The desire for more depth and meaning came from our very core. You can't fight that. When life becomes monotonous, you know you need to make a change. We craved more of life, knowing that there was so much more to learn and experience. We wanted less of the repetitive menial chaos and more of what resonated with us. We were mindful of our goals and what we wanted our lives to look like.

Reality Is What You Make It

Every decision you make today is creating your future, and your thoughts and intentions are creating your reality. How often have you heard someone say they're "back to reality" after returning home from a vacation? They make it sound as if it's a bad thing, right? It is as if they don't like their life. Does that sound like someone living with intention? Some may just be repeating a well-known saying, not giving any thought to the idea that they may actually be sabotaging themselves when they say that. The truth is, reality is what you make it.

Most fail to realize that making just a few simple changes can actually change the direction of their lives. It's true! You can absolutely transform your reality into something beautiful, rewarding, and exactly what you want your life to look like. But you have to design it that way. You may be thinking, *How do I do that?* Well, you have to match the frequency with the reality that you want. Study the universal laws, become consciously aware of your thoughts, and be willing to give yourself a command and follow it. If you're just drifting through life making no attempt to change, expand, or improve, then the proof will be in the results depicting your reality. Your reality is a direct reflection of your vibration.

For me, the main objective is to live my best life and to make the greatest amount of progress toward my dreams and goals. Goals will actually usher intentionality into your life. For years, I neglected to live a life that I loved, and during that time I didn't even really have any goals, but that was the reality I created for myself. I take full responsibility for that. This sweeping realization permanently shifted my perception. Today, by making intentional decisions to be involved in the outcomes of my life, I have created a new reality, loving life and doing exactly what I want to do. If you are running from your life, then a week away on the beach won't change anything. Upon your return you'll just be faced with the same life you temporarily escaped from.

Ask, Believe, Receive

Life has so much more meaning and is less superficial since I made a clear decision to live intentionally. It caused my husband and I to think deeply about how we wanted to live our lives. We must pattern ourselves to not only talk the talk, but to walk the walk. This became evident to me when I sat across from him one day and said, "I want to build a new home." At first, he looked at me with a slight look of confusion on his face, and I politely repeated myself with sincerity in my voice. "I *really* want to build a new home." The home we lived in was absolutely beautiful, but it did not serve our needs any longer. We were both so different from who we were when we first built it back in 2004.

Although my statement took him by surprise, I could tell he was really beginning to think about the possibility of building a new home or at least considering to move. After a moment of silence, he started dreaming out loud and we shared our ideas about what we both wanted. In that moment we realized we were settling for a home that neither one of us truly wanted to live in any longer. That's not intentional living. Intentional living supports making decisions that are congruent with the life you see yourself living. It promotes living in a way that you get the most out of life by doing the things you love. When you keep your eye on the prize, you tend to forget about all the other distractions and focus only on what matters most to you.

We started planning our next move. All we knew was that we wanted to live where our every desire would be fulfilled. We also started to travel more and had a strong desire to meet new people, develop meaningful friendships, and spend quality time with our family. Everything we desired fell right into place for us. It was simply magical to watch the entire process unfold. Looking back, I now realize this occurred through three important steps:

1. Ask
2. Believe
3. Receive

Since we did this, a whole new world has opened up right before our eyes. It didn't take long for us to learn how to relax into the moment while aligning ourselves with those things we loved to do, and with what is most important to us.

Intention Is Waking Up and Smelling the Coffee

While visiting with a few of my colleagues, we discussed negative habitual patterns and how they can keep one from thriving and living an intentional life. Living from intention and less out of habit is truly fulfilling to the soul. And then, as we live from the fulfilled soul, life begins to unfold in many beautiful ways.

Sophia shared a story with us about how her sister, Maria, was stuck in a job that she did not like while having big dreams of owning her own business one day. Maria had been gainfully employed with the same company since she was in her early twenties, which was over twenty-two years ago. She often expressed fear of change, and even though she settled for a job that sucked the life out of her, she continued to work there for years. Her biggest interest was her retirement. It would be twenty years before she could retire. She depended on that money to then fulfill the dream of opening her own business and traveling the world, especially a trip to Italy.

Sophia encouraged Maria to step out of her comfort zone and intentionally pursue the dreams that were speaking to her heart right now, today, instead of waiting for her retirement in twenty years. Reluctantly, Maria started dreaming and shared her ideas and desires with her husband, Joseph. After deep thought and much consideration, Maria put in her resignation, and she and Joseph mortgaged their home to open a quaint little coffee café.

Maria and Joseph joyfully served the community that they loved and cherished. Sophia explained how fascinating it was to watch them work together and elaborated on how it takes a certain type of couple to be able to work and live together 24/7. Their coffee café was well known by the locals, and they made many new friends. They had a contagious energy, as they were both so happy in their element. It was a dream come true to own their own business and to spend so much time together. Because they had the desire to get more out of life, together, they took that leap of faith and went after their dreams while supporting each other's ideas. Their coffee café was very successful. It afforded them a life that they had only dreamed about in the past.

Sophia explained that eight years into the business Maria became ill, and she relied on Sophia to step in and help pick up the slack. With a look of sorrow, she shared that it just wasn't the same without her sister being there. The energy in the café was somber. Joseph spent most of his time with his wife, trying to nurse her back to health. One evening Sophia received a phone call from Joseph, and as he wept, he shared the news that Maria had unexpectedly passed away—they had all thought she was well on her way to recovery. She'd had dreams of traveling the world and thought that one day she would dabble in all the hobbies that brought her so much joy.

Joseph didn't dwell on the lost opportunities. Rather, he focused on what they had gained by *seizing the moment* and opening the coffee café. It was Maria's idea that allowed them to intentionally be together for the last eight years of their lives. Through his tears, Joseph said it was the best eight years of his life. They enjoyed a sense of freedom doing what they loved and being in the moment with each other day in and day out. His wife never expected to die so soon. After all, they were going to travel the world together. They had not yet made that special trip to Italy, and Maria didn't know that Joseph was secretly planning a celebratory trip for their ten-year anniversary of being in business together.

All we have is today. Living intentionally respects that notion. If Maria had not made the decision to pursue her dream of owning a business when she did, she would have continued to work for the last eight years of her life in an environment she did not enjoy. Her dream of owning her own business would have died along with her that day. And to think she wanted to wait until she retired before pursuing her lifelong dream.

This story should serve as an example and motivation to find it within yourself to live an intentional life. I don't want you to look back and say *I wish I did*. I want you to look back and say *I'm glad I did*. We don't know how long we have on this earth, and the trajectory of your life will greatly depend on the decisions you make, starting today.

Once Your Vision Changes, Your Life Changes

As you harness the amazing power of intentional living, you will reap the benefits of living your life in a way that is most important to you. Vivid clarity of your dreams and goals will begin to surface as well as a more mindful approach to life. As you get reacquainted with your truth and with what matters most to you, it will become much easier to identify how you truly want to live. Once your vision changes, your life changes. Allow the vision to engulf you as you live with intention. Essentially, your vision becomes your why. Stand firm on what you want your life to resemble. Embracing intentional living causes one to gain a renewed sense of appreciation for life and the world they live in.

Loving Reminders:

- ♥ Core values are the foundation for intentional living.
- ♥ Your vision should embody your core values.
- ♥ Examine the flow of your life.
- ♥ Attitude is everything.
- ♥ Stop and smell the roses.
- ♥ Your reality is a direct reflection of your vibration.
- ♥ Goals will actually usher intentionality into your life.
- ♥ Intentional living supports making decisions that are congruent with the life you see yourself living.
- ♥ Once your vision changes, your life changes.

SEVEN

CREATING A LIFE THAT YOU LOVE

Intention is the starting point of your dreams, and now that you're living with intention, you are making a commitment to yourself to live a life that *gives* you life. Life and all its wonders are much more fruitful when you take action from a place of aligned clarity. There may be moments when you feel challenged; just remember to return to your truth and what matters most to you. Intention is the starting point of your dreams. When you move away from old habits that are not serving you and form new habits that do, with conscious thought backed by intent, you will be well on your way to creating a life that you love.

As you continue on your transformational journey, you will be relentless in peeling back the layers of life that are standing in your way. Many new truths will reveal themselves. Take notice. One of the main lessons I've learned throughout my studies has been the power of awareness. You must become consciously aware of the life you desire before you can consciously create a life that you love. We all have areas in our lives that we want to expand in or improve upon spiritually, financially, physically, relationally, and professionally. Give your life the attention it so deserves.

Dare to Dream

Creating a life you love is going to require continued imagination, action, and dedication on your part. Your future is of your own making. Dare to dream beyond the reality you have currently created for yourself. Keep in mind that we live in an abundant universe. Once you truly understand this and properly apply the universal laws, your dreams will go from the invisible realm to the physical realm. But it all begins with one question that you must ask yourself: What would I really love?

Yes! What would you *really* love? Open yourself up and imagine the possibilities that may lead you on the path to discovering your best life and personal freedom. Notice that spark in your imagination. There it is, your dream permeating the invisible. You smile and imagine for a moment that you are living your dream in all areas of life. And that's how it's done. All too often I hear of people chasing their dreams as if the dream is out there somewhere. You don't have to chase anything. Your dreams are inside of you.

To bring your dream into manifestation, you must move from your dream living inside of you to acting as if you have already achieved it. This is Universal Law 101. Even if your dream doesn't seem logical, dream it anyway. Bob Proctor clearly states, "Don't let logic stop you. If you've got the dream and you're emotionally involved with the idea, it must move into form." When you are on the frequency of the dream you are holding in your mind, you may *think* you have an idea of how that dream will come into form, but then God reveals the answer to you in a way that you least expected. I love when that happens! You see, our radar is focused on what's right in front of us, but really we have no idea when, where, or even how the blessings will come. You have to remember that you are dealing with the *infinite*. There is a life force flowing to you and through you, waiting to express itself through *your dreams*. You are the physical expression of the omnipotent God. Omni = all and Potent = powerful. God is your infinite supply.

If you could live each day following your passion, what would that look like to you? Close your eyes and visualize a life that you would love. With no circumstances or limitations holding you back, allow yourself to dream freely as you used to do when you were a child full of excitement. Now begin to describe it out loud from beginning to end. What does your perfect day look like? Better yet, what does it *feel* like? Remember, the feeling is the secret. Feeling is conscious awareness of vibration. Some may find it difficult to do this because their deep-seated conditioned beliefs actively block them from dreaming freely. For example, many people don't perceive themselves as worthy of their dream. They think, *What good would it do to dream of a life I would love when things like that don't happen to people like me?*

If this is your thinking, then your very own thoughts are blocking your growth. To create a life that you love, you must be willing to get out of your own way, especially if you want to fulfill your dreams, expand in life, and live with intention. You have the ability to change your perception of anything. It is simply a choice. Amazing things don't just happen to other people, amazing things can happen to you too.

Believing Is Seeing

If you don't have any idea where you see yourself in five years or even ten years from now, then chances are you will be exactly where you are today. The paradigm encourages you to live a small life, allowing circumstances to stop you before you even get started. It's very common for people to assess their self-worth according to their circumstances, such as, *I lost my job! I'm such a loser.* Life does not always go according to plan, and you will need to be able to separate yourself from who you are and what has happened to you. In fact, if you do lose your job, celebrate! This just means you are completely free to find a better job or start your own business. You may even consider that as a huge nudge for you to do more with your life.

Stop your inner critic in its tracks and reclaim your thoughts. Be bold! Remind yourself that you are better than any negative thoughts. Your incessant mind chatter will keep you from achieving your dreams, but only if you allow it. When the mind is full of turbulence, you are unable to make clear decisions. Claim new positive thoughts and repeat them aloud in a voice that demands and captures your attention. Shake those other thoughts off. Tap into the Infinite Intelligence as your resource and remain connected. Remember, there is a power within you that is far greater than any circumstance or situation on the outside. It's not seeing is believing, it's believing is seeing.

A Burning Desire

While using the Law of Specificity, you will need to identify clearly what you want to achieve. Get specific about your goals. These goals should consist of what you want, not what you think you can achieve. It doesn't get any clearer than that. If you only focus on what you think you can achieve, then you are justifying your future results and will end up settling for less. If you have huge dreams and goals, honor them. They are inside of you for a reason, and you are certainly worthy of them. You don't need to know how you will achieve your goals, but you do need to create a definite plan of action for carrying out your desires.

Desire is the key word here. Desire is the starting point of all achievement. If you truly desire to create a life that you love, then you better have a burning desire to make it happen. You can't just wish for change. You have to be willing to choose a definite goal and place all of your energy and effort behind it. Your state of mind is essential to your success. What can you do right now in the interest of your dream? What is the first step you can take?

I have a suggestion for you. Write out your goal as if it has already manifested. Bob and Sandy faithfully encourage writing out your goal in the present tense. You can't just claim you want plenty of money, you must be clear and concise. In reading your goal card

94

aloud, you should see it in your mind's eye and feel it in every cell of your body as if you are already in possession of the dream. In doing so you are communicating the object of your desire directly to your subconscious mind in the spirit of faith. You mustn't lose the connection of the energetic frequency of experiencing your desired dream. Continue to live in the expectation of it.

Begin your goal card with these powerful words: I am so happy and grateful now that…

Fill in the rest, be specific about your goal, and choose your words with fastidious care. Remember to write it out as if the goal has already been achieved.

Decisions, Decisions

An excellent habit to master is making decisions promptly. Every decision you make is shaping your life, so give careful thought to your choices and make sure they are in alignment with who you are. If it doesn't feel right, then it's not right. Learn to recognize those feelings. Stop trying to force things to happen; forcing negates. Some feel as if making a decision is paralyzing, but you know what's really paralyzing? Looking back on your life and realizing all of the missed opportunities that were right there in front of you. By avoiding decisions, you are doing yourself a disservice. It would be unrealistic to create a life that you love if you aren't willing to make decisions that support it. This is why so many are living an unfulfilled life. They struggle with making decisions.

When we listen to our negative self-talk, we sometimes make ourselves believe it is far easier to just stay where we are rather than make tough decisions. Have you ever noticed how many people struggle with even the smallest of decisions? The Law of Polarity states that everything has a polar opposite, and the opposite of decision is procrastination. Being stuck in that frame of mind can be quite disappointing now and only amplified later in life. There's a huge disconnect for many as they swim in a sea of self-doubt and remain unmotivated about life, all because they can't make a decision and have allowed logical thinking and conditioned-based thoughts to take over, which causes them to forfeit their dreams.

On the other hand, decision making can be fun. It's all an attitude of the mind. Your decisions today shape your destiny tomorrow. Decide today that you are ready to step into your power. Decide today that you are ready to live your life in a way that has more meaning. Decide today that you are ready to claim this very moment in time for yourself. Decide today that you are worthy of change, and that you will no longer settle for a life that does not give you life.

Mindset Matters

The mind is constantly inflicted with a barrage of thoughts. It's like the water we swim in—over time, we get used to it. It's just become a way of life. We've gotten so used to the struggle or the numbing of the mind that we think this is it, life as we know it. But understand that your mindset matters in every aspect of your life. If you are defeated in your thoughts, you will be defeated in your life. Look around; does your life resemble the same life even just a year ago? Don't you desire a better life for yourself and your family? Of course you do. And although it is exciting to want a better life for yourself, you cannot push your will on someone else. As admirable as your feelings and thoughts are for the other person, they must want it for themselves, otherwise it won't be sustainable. Everyone holds a unique vision of themselves and the life they want to live. Creating a life that you love depends on your ability to change the way you think. By understanding the Law of Perpetual Transmutation, you should have a clear understanding of how your habitual thinking is either moving you backward or forward—there is no in-between.

You have the power to change your life's results and your emotional state simply by changing the way you think. You absolutely have the capacity to choose one thought over another; you just have to be willing to do so. You get a really good idea about what's going on inside of someone's mind by the results in their lives. Results don't lie.

Most people, and I used to be one of them, have not even studied themselves enough to know what they are capable of doing. Instead of creating a life that they love, most have been too easily persuaded to give up by their own thinking. All too often people will identify themselves as their own negative thoughts. That's exactly what happened to me. My negative habitual tendencies interfered with my personal advancement in life. But when you change your thoughts, you change your life as a result. And, just like me, I believe there will come a time for you when you interrupt your old way of thinking and replace it with a completely new thought pattern, one that encourages real and lasting change. Until you do, you will continue to manifest your current circumstances. Simply put, your conditions will never change if your thoughts never change. The rest of your life will ultimately reflect the way you think. So if you want to create a life that you love, you must be willing to change the way you think.

Internal Enemies

Every internal enemy is directly linked to your mindset. You may recognize these traps as old familiar patterns of thought that have hindered your growth and the progression of your dreams. Although many of them can be quite challenging to overcome, it is imperative that you find the strength and courage to master them. If you don't master these internal enemies, chances are you will continue to live your life by default rather than by design.

1. **Comfort zone:** Not willing to grow and expand the mind. This is one of the most common traps that many people create for themselves.

2. **Excuses:** Justifying why you haven't moved forward, whether it's blaming yourself or others.

3. **Denial:** Can't fix what you don't admit to.

4. **Lack of self-awareness:** Unaware of your infinite potential.

5. **Procrastination:** Unable to make decisions.

6. **Playing the victim role:** Poor me. Look what happened to me.

7. **Jealousy:** Envious of others.

8. **Living in lack:** If you are living and operating out of lack, you are only inviting more lack into your life. Where attention goes energy flows. So if you are constantly complaining about what you don't have, you are only inviting more of the same.

9. **Fear:** Being driven by fear will only paralyze you, your thoughts, and your dreams.

10. **Guilt:** It's difficult to enjoy life when there is an accumulation of guilt.

11. **Judgment:** When judgment is cast, it is of one's own personal opinion and not that of a necessary truth.

12. **Comparison:** Someone will always have more than you and someone will always have less than you. Don't play the comparison game.

You may not even be aware that these internal enemies are affecting your life. Take a closer look. Remember, honesty is key. I hid behind many of these traps for years. The layers of causation were many. To truly create a life that you love, you must be willing to break through the confines of your mind.

The Tug-of-War Within

I was cautious for many years. I took the logical approach and allowed my circumstances to hold me back as I tiptoed through life, playing it small. I worked in our family business for over twenty years, and even though the business was growing and my life was advancing beautifully, my own personal dreams and desires were not. They weren't going to advance on their own, as wishing isn't willing. I think so many people have dreams, but just like me, they suppress them and place them on the back burner.

Although my contribution to the business was significant and I enjoyed working with my husband, the reality is I was trading my life for something I no longer desired to do. I was fading away, and all I wanted to do was leap forward in fullness and excitement. I craved to be in an atmosphere that was in harmony with my creative abilities. I didn't realize the burden I carried by staying there for so long and how it truly affected my life. I say this with the utmost love and respect, as our family business has served us well over the years, but it just wasn't my dream, it was my husband's. He successfully created a life that he loved, while I lived with longing and discontent.

As much as my husband wanted me to work with him, I also felt an obligation to help and support him. That obligation was a diversion tactic that my ego used to keep me in my comfort zone. I became a servant to my illusionary thoughts and was in serious need of inner reflection. By succumbing to fear, I allowed it to dictate the outcome of my life, and even though I wanted more out of life, I sat on the sidelines disconnected from myself, unfulfilled and secretly dwelling on my own pity party. When you are disconnected from your authentic self, it's easy to blame outside circumstances. I did that for years. But the truth is I failed to focus on making the decisions that would lead me to creating a life that I loved. That life would only appear through the expansion of self.

Thankfully, over the course of many years I became aware of the pull from Spirit to do something new, something that resonated with me. It is strictly up to you to recognize the pull and to use it as a catalyst for changes in your life. Awareness is key. While the human part of me agreed to put my dreams on hold, the spiritual part encouraged me to move forward. Have you ever experienced that before? It felt like a tug-of-war within, but once I finally made the decision to move in the direction of my dreams, I immediately felt at peace. The struggle subsided as the built-up resistance faded away. I may have lost sight of my goal from time to time, but I never lost sight of my dream.

In order to move forward in alignment, I had to relinquish my controlling qualities and believe that someone could do my job just as well if not better than I could. Abandoning caution, I moved full speed ahead. I hired someone within our company to take over my position, and I am grateful it was a successful transition. I have never looked back. Once I made the decision to hire someone, everything started to fall into place. That's how it works. The divine synchronicities of the universe kicked in. It's like the universe was patiently waiting for me to make a decision and take action.

Today I am emotionally attached to and involved in what I am doing with my life. I am happy, I am fulfilled, and I am grateful that I took the leap. Don't get stuck thinking that you need to know every detail of your life and how it will unfold. Just take one small step at a time and trust the process. I now wake up every single day full of excitement and gratitude knowing that I have created an environment that is 100 percent conducive to my dreams, while I remain in alignment with my heart and fulfill my lifelong desires. I share this with you not to impress you but to press upon you that once you take the first step through the invisible boundary in your mind, you will begin to create a life that you love as well.

You Attract What You Are

How many people have jumped at the first opportunity to take a job right out of high school or college just to pay the bills, only to find themselves unfulfilled in the same place many years later? They don't have a job, that job has them. When you have created a life that you love, you jump out of bed in the morning full of zest for life. And if you're not, then you aren't in harmony with the life you are living. You are simply going through the motions. I did that for many years.

Because we all essentially trade our lives for a job, we should ask ourselves if the job is worthy of us, not if we are worthy of the job. The Law of Sacrifice states that you must give up something in order to get something. If you are going to sacrifice your entire life for a job or career, make sure it's one that you love. Think about all the hours you have invested in what you call your life. How often have you spoken about how fast the years have zipped by, or how you secretly wish you had pursued a certain dream, career, or lifestyle that reflects the image you have held in your mind for years, but didn't. Let me assure you, you aren't the only one.

I met someone a long time ago who was struggling in every aspect of his life. His marriage fell apart, money was scarce, he owned a beat-up old car, and he could never seem to get ahead in life. Every day was a repeat of the day before—a pure struggle. While we lost touch, I ran into him at least ten years later. Nothing had changed. That was a huge eye-opener for me, and it made me take a deeper look within. Nothing had changed in my life either as far as my dreams were concerned. I yearned to create a life that I loved, and in that moment I realized you don't attract what you want, you attract what you are.

Because I was fearful and full of doubt, my dreams sat dormant waiting for me to take action. You see, what you want comes from conscious thinking, and what you are comes from your subconscious thinking. Your subconscious thinking is where all your paradigms are stored. Hence, "As a man thinketh, so is he." You can only attract to you what you are in harmony with. If you are in harmony with lack, then you will attract lack. If you are in harmony with wealth, then you will attract wealth.

Protecting Your Dreams

Owning your story can be difficult, but it is not nearly as difficult as hiding from it. I know about that all too well. I learned to increase the richness in all areas of my life by celebrating it in ways that were meaningful to me. As you celebrate in ways that are meaningful to you, you will begin to feel expanded in the presence of your ideas. Allow the brilliant design of the images in your mind to reflect your every desire. This is your time. Jump in, roll up your sleeves, and start creating a life that you absolutely love. Champion your dreams. Protect them and hold them in the highest vibration. Remember, you had a dream before anyone had an opinion. You may want to write a book, open a business, purchase an art gallery, or even sail around the world. Give yourself permission to dream, and speak of them only to the ones who will give you encouragement.

When something speaks to your heart, listen. Pay very, very close attention. If you're not careful, the ego will dominate the spirit. When we let go and understand that God is in control, this magnificent Universal Intelligence will reveal itself. So don't you worry about what other people think because *it's not their calling, it's yours*, and the only opinion that matters is yours and yours alone. You are going to discover that everyone has been raised with their own set of beliefs and their own set of paradigms. They will be quick to shower you with what they think is socially acceptable. If everyone allowed what other people thought to interfere with their calling or their dreams, the world would never evolve. Today we would not have electricity, personal computers, automobiles, or even be able to take a flight, and so much more which has advanced our society. The world has come this far because of the ones who dared to dream *boldly*.

One of the most important lessons you will learn while creating the life that you love is to be very protective of your dreams. Be very selective who you share them with. Not everyone will be interested in seeing you advance, change, or even succeed in life. Keep in mind that how people perceive you may have more to do with them rather than you. They may see something in you that they don't see in themselves, making them feel threatened, competitive, envious, judgmental, and even distant. We are all so different and everyone has his own mind chatter going on. But it is your responsibility alone to just focus on what you are doing and tune out the naysayers. Just remember, the advice that most people share with you will come from their own level of awareness and their own set of paradigms.

The universe is ready to give you what you are in harmony with. The desires of your heart are meant to manifest, but you must take action. In this fast-paced world it's easy to get lost in what you don't want; creating a life that you love enables you to focus on what you do want. As you learn to stand in your power and live in your truth, you will no longer allow your life to be controlled by the false belief you once held of yourself. Wake up and honor who you are and your own divine individuality. Listen to what your heart is whispering to you. Put a plan of action together and create a life that you will absolutely love. By doing so you are positioning yourself for growth. Don't get hung up on searching for your life's purpose, just start living on purpose.

Loving Reminders:

- ♥ Give your life the attention it so deserves.
- ♥ Dare to dream beyond the reality you have currently created for yourself.
- ♥ Even if your dream doesn't seem logical, dream it anyway.
- ♥ Tap into Infinite Intelligence as your resource and remain connected.
- ♥ Desire is the starting point of all achievement.
- ♥ You can only attract to you what you are in harmony with.
- ♥ Celebrate your life in ways that are meaningful to you.
- ♥ Champion your dreams.
- ♥ When something speaks to your heart, listen.
- ♥ The desires of your heart are meant to manifest.
- ♥ Wake up and honor who you are and your own divine individuality.
- ♥ Just start living on purpose.

EIGHT

FORGIVENESS:
THE GIFT YOU GIVE TO YOURSELF
AND OTHERS

Your dreams will unleash limitless possibilities of the life you so desire. Committing to making a positive shift in your daily habits, choices, and attitude will inevitably evoke sustained success and freedom in creating a life that you love. As you navigate your way through new levels of freedom, it is essential to consciously extend forgiveness. You must possess the willingness to relinquish anything that does not support your vision of living your best life.

The secret to unlocking the present moment is surrendering venomous built-up resentments. Forgiveness is love in action and is a vital component to living your best life as a whole. As your life expands, you will encounter many layers of lessons. Practicing forgiveness is one of those many layers. I believe the challenges we endure and the people we meet throughout our lifetime are lessons that serve our soul's growth. While forgiveness is not naturally woven into the hearts of everyone, it is an essential practice for us all.

I have learned that forgiving someone who has hurt me only expands the depth and freedom I possess within. It has helped me to become more compassionate, open, and understanding. I'm sure you've experienced the expansive power of forgiveness through many facets, whether it was forgiving yourself, forgiving others, or receiving forgiveness from someone else. Forgiveness requires work, but most importantly it requires love. While it can be a sensitive subject, it offers each of us the opportunity to heal, make amends, and move forward. Consider how your emotional and physical well-being are at stake. As a result, each of us has our own work to do. We are all capable of forgiveness.

By choosing to forgive, you'll reap the benefit of moving forward with endless opportunities for resolution. Occurrences that once dominated your thoughts eventually become nonexistent, and you'll have no desire to look back. The reciprocal is also true. By choosing not to forgive, you may become a prisoner of your own mind, oppressed with memories of the past. Stored-up negative memories are all playing an essential part in affecting your health and your everyday living.

So that begs the question: Which will you choose?

What You Resist Persists

A vital part of my shift came through extending real forgiveness, not fake forgiveness where you pretend to forgive but secretly hold a grudge. I began to let things roll off my back. I no longer took things for granted. I started minding my own business, and I began to see people in a different light. In fact, I began to see their light. What I desired most was to put forth a true conscious effort in authentic forgiveness and live from this transformative state. Approaching life with grace helped me transform my thinking. While being inten-tional in extending forgiveness toward others and myself, I felt the negative energy subside. We should all strive for this. No one wants to consciously remain stuck in bitterness and hatred. The truth is, what you resist persists. I am determined to live my greatest life, and the journey demands my own willingness to forgive. I want to help you accomplish the same.

When a person or event has caused agitation, view it as a lesson for you, not an opportunity to find fault in what the other did wrong. I know this may ruffle a few feathers, but trust me, if you are agitated, then something is going on inside of you. I am not saying dismiss what the offender did, I am simply suggesting that you look deep within to see what set you off. Many will ardently dismiss people from their lives without even looking inside themselves to see what needs to be healed. There are layers and layers of valuable lessons everywhere; you just have to be willing to learn from them.

As flawed as you may think the other person is, remember, what you see in others you also see in yourself. Everyone is your mirror reflecting parts of your own consciousness back to you. I was in total disbelief when I first learned of the Law of Reflection, but once I removed my ever so faithful ego I began to understand. I started to pay attention to everyone who came in and out of my life, and I asked, *What might this reflection be teaching me?* The universe has a way of allowing us to repeat the same spiritual lessons during our time here on earth until we inevitably learn from them. I am so grateful that I am now able to face my own spiritual lessons with humility.

Make Peace with Your Past

Guilt is a way of negatively judging ourselves. It depletes us, which consequently leads to feelings of inadequacy. Some may experience embarrassment and become withdrawn. The only way out is to own up to what you have done. Guilt is a powerful emotion that negatively affects one's ability to move forward in life if left unattended.

Has something been gnawing at your heart? Have you magnified an offense in your mind? Did you recently lie to a friend? Are you still beating yourself up because of the way you raised your children? Were you fired over a senseless act, causing your entire family to suffer? Did you waste your parents' money by flunking out of college? Each of these experiences can leave one feeling guilty and in need of forgiveness.

Guilt can have an enormous effect on your life, and your daily mind chatter is a frequent reminder. It may be the culprit to what's holding you back or causing you to feel unhappy and unworthy. You don't have to believe everything you think. It is crucial to forgive yourself of current and past mistakes. Dwelling on failure will only intensify guilt and continuing to punish yourself will only intensify your pain. Instead of focusing on what you cannot change, focus on what you can. Shift your unproductive painful thoughts toward a more positive mental attitude. Have compassion for yourself. Sometimes it's much easier to forgive others than oneself. I'm not saying let yourself off the hook; it's important to admit when you have done wrong. But life goes on, and it will. So should you.

Many will unknowingly sabotage themselves by holding onto negative feelings. This creates suffering in many or all areas of life, spiritually, financially, physically, relationally, and professionally. By making peace with your past and reclaiming your thoughts, you are consciously setting the intention to heal as you grow through the adversity of your guilt and pain. Self-forgiveness is a powerful form of self-love. It is a gift you give to yourself. We can only extend to others what we are willing to extend to ourselves. Peace of mind is priceless. Your relationship with others will improve, and most importantly the relationship you have with yourself will improve. Your incessant mind chatter will be replaced with emotional healing as you lovingly bestow gentle waves of forgiveness.

Allow Forgiveness

For many, the mere whisper of the word forgive challenges the ego heavily. Usually the first response is to seek out revenge to justify the pain or sadness in one's life. Some wear their hearts on their sleeves and some wear their hatred. Believe it or not, some will refuse to forgive and hold onto their pain as if they'll receive an award for doing so. It allows them to feel miserable and still hold the blame over the offender's head. This way they are able to hold the offender hostage by way of blaming them for their unhappiness, when in all actuality we are responsible for our own happiness. Don't give that power to someone else. Forgiveness is a learned practice, and one of the hardest things I've encountered was giving up the power to continue to punish the other person in my mind. It was wise to send them love and move on instead.

It can be especially painful if we've been hurt by someone we love and trust. Perhaps someone has unleashed their anger purely out of confusion, a misunderstanding, or even suppressed hurt feelings. Human beings are going to make mistakes. They will fall short of your expectations at some point in life. As you move forward in the days ahead, ask yourself these questions:

- Could I possibly be overreacting?
- Does the sentence I've given the offender fit the perceived crime?
- Is there an opportunity for reconciliation?
- Would I desire forgiveness if I made the same mistake?

Allow someone to right the wrong they have committed. Listen with an open heart and an open mind. Agree to disagree if you must, but you've got to reveal it to heal it. People are not perfect, and they will do things to upset you. Remember what it feels like to be on the receiving end of forgiveness. Accept the faults of others just as you would have them to be accepting of yours. Everyone has faults. Forgiving someone doesn't mean you have to forget what happened unless you choose to. But allowing yourself to forgive someone who has hurt you both intentionally and unintentionally will free you from constantly reliving the pain. Trust your ability. When was the last time you truly, deeply forgave someone?

While everyone is on their own path, you have the ability to make your own decisions. Sit with the deepest depths of your brokenness.

Stop reburying the pain; feelings just want to be felt. Take the time to properly heal and process your emotions. Just because this may be a part of your existence today doesn't mean it has to be a part of your existence tomorrow. Your thinking and your willingness to forgive will determine that.

Forgiveness is tough, but oh so liberating. It has been said that the ones closest to you or the ones who mean the most to you are the ones who can hurt you the deepest. Let me clarify, the other person cannot hurt you. It is the expectation you have attached to the relationship that causes the hurtful feelings, and we ordinarily confuse the two. By having an interest and attachment to the outcome of the conflict, hurtful feelings arise.

Many have a paradigm around forgiveness. The paradigm says you hurt me and I have to make you pay—for the rest of your life and even after you die. I understand that sometimes it just feels so empowering to hold a grudge and refuse to forgive someone, as I have been there myself, but it is a gut-wrenching experience. People who hold grudges are more inclined to bring up past experiences for the sake of getting attention and with the hopes of getting others to choose sides. That is pure ego taking center stage.

It's unfortunate how a lifetime of memories can sometimes be superseded by assumptions, mistakes, or misunderstandings all because ego has been allowed to take over. We miss the opportunity for reconciliation by way of feeding our own pain. We create our own suffering when we obsess over past hurtful experiences. You can greatly influence the outcome of your life by starting with forgiveness. I've endured hardships in my life, and choosing forgiveness is what healed my soul. There's a calmness underneath the surface of all chaos; you just have to be willing to get into harmony with it.

At times my ego didn't want to expose its vulnerability in order to forgive someone. But by not allowing myself to extend forgiveness I was just setting myself up to carry the burden, and I am not willing to spend my life that way any longer. I will carry people in my heart even if I'm not in theirs. I no longer feel the need to perpetuate negative life patterns by not being the one who is willing to forgive. That's how my wall was built in the first place, so instead I choose to access love and extend forgiveness today.

Lessons Learned

There are lessons to learn from every experience in life. I know this from my own experiences. Once I was able to see past my current life circumstances, every lesson I learned guided me toward a new path in life. Through careful navigation I began to feel more focused and fulfilled while creating a life that I loved. As hard as it was at times to embrace the many lessons, changes, and challenges that unfolded in what I thought were very dark times, I am grateful they eventually revealed themselves as the biggest blessings in my life. I viewed those blessings as confirmation of moving forward.

I forgave Gangsta Wendy for the times she was unable to extend love and embraced my own loving presence. This has allowed me to have healing, compassion, and forgiveness toward any past discrepancies I may have caused or endured personally. A victim consciousness can take on many forms, but choosing to release my pain allowed me to take the focus off myself and my own stories of victimization, and redirect it toward more positive areas in my life.

When you hold onto the identity of being wronged, you are missing out on opportunities to live in the present moment of life's new and rewarding experiences. Living that way will only disconnect you from love, compassion, and understanding, the very energies needed to forgive others. I can think of so many other ways I'd prefer to spend my time and energy. Being angry, holding a grudge, or continuously talking about negative past experiences is not one of them. You cannot change the past, but you can change your future experiences by what and how you think today.

I believe that each experience we endure (good, bad, or indifferent) unfolds as a gift even though it may not seem that way at first. In fact, the ones who have caused the most pain and have proven to be the most difficult should be viewed as our greatest teachers and most sacred friends. Even if those relationships go awry and take a disastrous turn, the key to maximizing your experience with them is to be open and aware of the lessons they offered. I'm sure this will give you a great deal to think about. Here's a sweet story about how a simple gesture of forgiveness could have changed everything:

Recently, while I was traveling through Madrid, several people piled into the elevator at the airport. An elderly man accidentally bumped into a young woman, causing her to lose her balance a bit just as the doors were closing. No harm was done, as I witnessed the entire process with my own eyes. He apologized by saying, "*Lo siento*," but she wanted nothing to do with him or his apology. I could tell she was quite annoyed, and she made sure everyone else knew it too as she exhaled ever so loudly. Her energy sucked the life right out of that elevator! The elevator doors opened, and she flung her way out while the rest of us continued to the next floor. We were still packed in there like sardines, and my eyes met with those of the elderly man. He smiled at me, and I gave him the biggest smile right back. I just felt awful for him. If I could have moved my arms I probably would have hugged him. I'm notorious for hugs. We didn't even speak the same language, but no one can mistake a smile.

Forgiveness exudes love. Love for myself and love for others. We were all strangers just trying to get through this thing called life and a crowded elevator ride. A simple that's okay offered as an extension of forgiveness from the young woman to the elderly man would have changed everything. Sadly, we have been conditioned to react a certain way to life's experiences. Conditioned to over exaggerate, conditioned to overreact, conditioned to overthink, conditioned to see the negative, and conditioned to get angry if someone accidentally bumps into us in an elevator. Forgiveness is at our disposal. It is readily available to extend at any moment in time. But like everything else, it takes a willingness to forgive.

By shifting your energy and your thinking, you will continue to peel back the old familiar patterns in the way you react, and over time you will form new habits of response with forgiveness automatically being one of them. That's exactly what happened to me. None of this is easy as you have your ego to contend with, but it is a choice. It will take time, and each experience is unique to itself, so treat each one accordingly and give forgiveness a chance. As time goes by, you will notice that your level of self-worth and your confidence in your new decision to forgive has gone up because you are now in control of your thoughts and feelings. Each one of us has the power to step up and show up in love and compassion, whether it be in a marriage, a friendship, a family relationship, or even a passing encounter with a person in the elevator.

Authentic Outlet

I pray there will come a time soon when you will be able to abandon any emotions that leave you with a disturbing, lasting effect on your life. Forgiveness should be used as an authentic outlet. Storms will come and go during your lifetime and learning how to control your actions will greatly depend on your thinking. We are all faced with many challenges, forgiveness being one of them, and not knowing what the outcome will be can be troubling at times. But God/Source/Universe/Spirit is omnipresent and knows the truth in every matter.

By utilizing the universal laws, all that has been done will inevitably be returned to you. Because the Law of Forgiveness ensures healing, the natural result will be peace of mind, body, and spirit. I'm sure most have heard the saying that forgiving others benefits you more than them. Well, I think forgiveness benefits everyone involved. I believe we are all connected for reasons only our own awareness levels can recognize. At some point in time, every marriage, every friendship, and every relationship will require some form of forgiveness.

Thus, how can you expect to be forgiven if you don't extend forgiveness to others? As we meet people along the way, we are all experiencing life lessons whether we realize it or not. I for one am not the same person I was yesterday. Each day I am growing, expanding, and evolving. Are you? It's important to understand that every vibration counts. Every single ripple. You and only you are responsible for the waves of energy that you send out into the world. Make sure they are kind, compassionate, and forgiving ones. May there be a time in your life when you are able to hold an image of yourself with a newfound perspective on forgiveness.

Loving Reminders

- ♥ Forgiveness is love in action.
- ♥ Forgiveness offers each of us the opportunity to heal, make amends, and move forward.
- ♥ We are all capable of forgiveness.
- ♥ What you resist persists.
- ♥ Everyone is your mirror reflecting parts of your own consciousness back to you.
- ♥ The universe has a way of allowing us to repeat the same spiritual lessons during our time here on earth until we inevitably learn from them.
- ♥ We can only extend to others what we are willing to extend to ourselves.
- ♥ Remember what it feels like to be on the receiving end of forgiveness.
- ♥ Feelings just want to be felt.
- ♥ There's a calmness underneath the surface of all chaos; you just have to be willing to get into harmony with it.

- ♥ There are lessons to learn from every experience in life.
- ♥ Forgiveness benefits everyone involved.
- ♥ You and only you are responsible for the waves of energy that you send out into the world.

NINE

LIVING IN A GRATEFUL STATE OF MIND

Forgiveness brings a new wave of energy as you allow every form of resentment to fade away. Although it may seem challenging it is necessary for growth. People who are grateful tend to be more forgiving. Inhale all the wonders of life and exhale gratitude, as it is an essential virtue to live by. By acknowledging and giving sincere thanks for everything in your life, you are opening a pathway for more.

As you come into harmony with the mindset of gratitude, the way you feel on the inside will begin to shift. A sense of peace and calm will encompass you. Gratitude is one of the highest emotional frequencies we can experience. Living in a grateful state of mind has opened the floodgates for all the good to enter into my life. When we are grateful for every opportunity that arises, we guarantee ourselves that life will undoubtedly send more opportunities our way.

I have always thought of myself as a grateful person, but I now have a better understanding of what it means to truly be grateful by seeing the effect gratitude has had in my life. Some days I'm just in awe and grateful to be alive. I've noticed the quality of my life has escalated to a new level since cultivating a deep sense of gratitude for everyone and everything. Gratitude is prayer in the highest form. Being grateful all the days of our lives is praying without ceasing. Gratitude, being an essential part of my shift, revealed an overflowing feeling of appreciation, love, and joy. I noticed that life was just all around more beautiful. That's what gratitude does, as it is a most powerful practice.

When I express gratitude, I am not declaring that my life is perfect by any means. We all experience the ebb and flow of life. What I am declaring is that I am fully aware of the blessings in my life. I have come face-to-face with difficulty, sadness, and grief. Believe me, there have been days when I didn't think I could muster an ounce of gratitude, but by being aware and recognizing that I have the power within to change my way of thinking, I now look for the good in every situation. That means even when there is only a speck of goodness or positivity, I latch onto it, and that's what I focus on. I then confidently move forward and express gratitude for the many lessons I have learned through every experience because I know firsthand the benefits of being grateful. It has changed my life for the better. I want to help you do the same.

Find the Good

I've often wondered, *Why aren't more people grateful?* Gratitude, being a core element of mindfulness, teaches one to appreciate what they have in the present moment. Most people aren't even living in the present moment. They're usually rushing around planning their next move, living in the past, or living in the future without consciously giving any regard to where they are right now. This causes one to miss out on the many blessings right in front of their eyes. It's easy to take things for granted during this practice.

Now, it's easy to be grateful when things are going your way, or when you're in perfect health, or when you are surrounded by the people you love. But when circumstances change gratitude is challenged in the minds and hearts of many. Living in a grateful state of mind is not about only being grateful for the positive experiences, it's about being grateful for all experiences. It's up to you to find the good in the challenges of your life. When the valley is deep and the light is dim, as difficult as it may seem, find something to be grateful for. Being disconnected from gratitude is detrimental to your health. It is most important to process the feelings of despair, pain, and hardship, as gratitude is not intended to cover up pain or difficulties, but it does serve as a reminder of all the good in one's life.

Why is it that many people are only grateful for the things in their lives when they are threatened with losing them, only then popping up out of nowhere declaring gratitude? What if you only received today what you were grateful for yesterday? In a world where most are likely to focus on the negative or where skepticism has been expressed toward finding the good, it may seem as if all hope has been lost. Life surely isn't without trials, and while many people identify with that, it outlines one's perception of life in the present moment as a negative. Yes, challenges can impede one's thinking, causing a person to focus only on the negative occurrences in life, but by consciously redirecting that energy toward living in gratefulness, you will help change your life for the better.

Attitude of Gratitude

Gratitude should be expressed as a pure thought. By cultivating an attitude of gratitude, you will not only live a more fulfilled and happy life, you will become an example to others. One by one, count your blessings and live in a grateful state of mind. Notice how each thought makes you feel. Expressing gratitude is good for the heart and can significantly impact a person's life. So get in the habit of expressing appreciation for every part of your life and start reaping the benefits today. Here are some of the many benefits of living with an attitude of gratitude. Notice how these positive effects will begin to transform your life:

- Lowers stress level
- Enhances kindness
- Produces better quality of sleep
- Increases productivity
- Magnifies your life experiences
- Helps you confidently overcome challenges
- Fosters an overall appreciation for life
- Lowers feelings of jealousy and envy
- Makes you more optimistic
- Boosts your mindset and physical well-being
- Causes you to be a beacon of light in dim situations
- Improves relationships (marriage, friendships, professional, etc.)
- Makes you more likely to pay it forward without expecting anything in return
- Raises your awareness level for the good others have bestowed upon you

But maybe most importantly, an attitude of gratitude makes you a happier human being. Keep up the great work! Each one of these benefits will only intensify as you continue to enhance your attitude of gratitude.

Avoiding Ingratitude

Sadly, there's ingratitude. Ingratitude is prevalent when you view yourself as lacking in life in some way, shape, or form. Simply being unhappy can unveil the sentiment of ingratitude. I've often stressed to others that gratitude is not only a state of being, it is also a moral sentiment. So there is obvious strife and conflict of thought jeopardizing the moral sentiment of gratitude when the heart and mind encounter ingratitude. People who live in a grateful state of mind, as opposed to those who exude ingratitude, have the capacity to find beauty in everything on their path. It's just a natural state of being for them.

How often have you performed a good deed for someone, and despite all of your help, they neglected to express their gratitude? A common response would be a simple yet heartfelt *thank you* as an expression of gratitude. Expressing gratitude doesn't always come easily for everyone. As the recipient of your generosity, some may feel ambiguous about what is expected or required of them. Others may have a sense of entitlement or may even feel as if your generosity is all quite unnecessary. Those who feel entitled will not adequately express gratitude. But none of these examples justifies ingratitude.

It has been my experience that when someone gives, they are cheerfully giving from the heart. But when there is no reciprocal expression of gratitude, as unintentional as it may be, it may leave the giver feeling a bit hurt or confused. I have been there myself, but I've learned to quiet my egoic mind and ask myself, *Am I really giving out of the goodness of my heart, or am I giving because I ex-pect or want something in return?* Part of being honest with your-self is being able to answer tough questions that have real meaning. You'll know if you've given yourself the correct answer because you will be in complete harmony with it. This is huge because many people don't even consider that thought. Instead they immediately allow the egoic mind to build a negative thought about the other person.

Just because it feels completely natural to you to express gratitude doesn't mean it will for others. Don't lose confidence in all of humanity simply because of the few who have exhibited ingratitude. One never truly knows what another is thinking, and as hard as it may be to believe, not everyone was taught to be grateful. They may not even be aware that their ingratitude is unexpressed gratitude. I bid you to look deep within your own heart when you encounter someone who treats you with ingratitude. Forgive them, send them love, and move on.

Remember, we don't usually set out to do something for someone just to get something in return, we do it out of the goodness of our hearts. There is a big difference between a transaction and interaction. Continue to give and be of service to others even if your efforts have not been appreciated by recent recipients of your good will. Just know that in your heart of hearts it will not go unnoticed.

Reset Your Mindset

Gratitude is a mindset. Use your time wisely and practice gratitude frequently. It doesn't have to be a long, drawn-out exercise. When you reset your mindset, you reset your life. Whew! Let's get back to being grateful. Did you notice a difference in your energy while you were reading about ingratitude? I sure did.

I've always loved the rain. And as I sit near a slightly raised window, I can hear the wind, rain, and thunder rolling in. A sense of gratitude completely fills me as I am reminded that I am home safe and sound doing what I love to do: writing. I love the fresh smell of rain, liquid sunshine, and I love the sound it makes as it lands on top of the water in the pool, resembling little jewels dancing around. On days like this it is calming and serene. I often welcome a rainy day because it rejuvenates me. It causes me to slow down, relax, and exhale. I am deeply grateful for days like this. I didn't always feel this way about the rain. But a shift in mindset allows me to see the beauty in it. What are some of the people, places, and things you are grateful for? I'm sure you can think of many.

By making a conscious effort to appreciate life and everything in it, you become filled with a positive energy source. Serenity and joyfulness immediately come to mind. Experiencing life and all its fullness in the present moment causes you to resist wanting to be anywhere else in your mind. The Law of Gratitude tells us that we should have an attitude of continuous praise and thanksgiving, and by being grateful for the smallest of things much will be received. Instead of focusing on not getting eight hours of sleep, try giving praise for the two hours you successfully achieved. Or, instead of complaining about going to work, be grateful that you have a job. Take what you have and build on it with praise, not negativity. Adopt a new vision and actively look for a solution. Being grateful is a choice, it's that simple. Look for the good. I promise you it's there. There are several ways to live a proactive life toward the betterment of life as a whole. They consist of:

- Writing in a daily gratitude journal. Decide on your preference of morning or evening. Find a quiet place, close your eyes, and take a deep breath in, exhale, and just start thinking about everything you are grateful for. People, places, things, circumstances, or solutions may all show up in your mind. Open your eyes and try to write down at least five to ten things. It has been said there's something very special about putting a pen to paper. In this case I find it to be not only a healing process but a transformative state of mind and body.

- Commit to finding ways to be grateful throughout your day. Treat it like a treasure hunt and consciously be on the lookout for things to be grateful for. Get your children involved and compare who found the most things to be grateful for during the day then share your findings during suppertime. It can be as simple as getting safely to and from your destination. Your warm cup of coffee or hot tea. The clothes you are wearing, your lunch date for the day, or even the laughs you've shared. Living in a grateful state of mind is easy once it becomes a daily habit.

- Serving others is not only rewarding, but it gives you a sense of gratitude to help someone out. It can be in any form. A smile, holding a door open, offering a lending hand, or a sincere hello can change a person's day. It's like saying, *I'm glad you're here; let me help you.* Showing that you genuinely care and want to help someone out is a gift in itself. Take the focus off yourself and extend it toward others.

- Leaving people with an impression of increase will not only leave them standing a little taller but smiling a little larger and feeling grateful they met you. When you leave someone with an impression of increase you are leaving them feeling better about themselves after spending time with you, more so than before they interacted with you. Give sincere compliments and look people in the eye, giving them your undivided attention. Be genuine and pass on good positive energy with everyone you come in contact with.

- Express your appreciation to others for the nice things they've said to you, done for you, or even made for you. By expressing gratitude, you are saying you respect the time and energy it took for them to do something for you. Explain to them how they made you feel. Share your positive experiences with them. Make it a point to write out a thank-you note, send an email, a text, flowers, or—here's an idea—pick up the phone and call them to express your gratitude for the difference they've made in your life.

I realize some of these exercises may seem very natural to you, while others may feel a bit forced or awkward at first. Just stick with them and soon they will become a part of who you are. Make a commitment to express daily gratitude, especially if you find yourself feeling sorry for yourself. There's no time like the present. Now is the perfect time to be grateful. Give it all you've got. Think of the overall impact gratitude would have on the world if everyone faithfully expressed gratitude. I think it's fascinating how any one of these exercises can positively affect your life. I recently had a heartfelt conversation with my dear friend Sirina about gratitude. Here is what she shared with me:

"My story begins in 1979 in a small town in Maine, where the summers meant that we finally got to enjoy the warm, sun-filled days swimming and riding bikes. I can remember riding my bike for miles, as long as we were within my mom's whistle distance when the street lights came on. It was fun to stay up late, and I loved to play hide-and-seek in the dark with all the neighborhood children. I cherish my memories and realize how lucky I am to have grown up in a time when the entire community looked after each other's children as if we were all one big family.

I was very familiar with the water. In fact, I loved it! I loved to hold my breath underwater as long as I could, only to try to hold it longer the next time. My mother would often grab me out of the water, frightened that I had been under for too long, and terrified that I was drowning as she herself could not swim. I faithfully watched a popular TV series based underwater. I was never afraid of the water and maybe a bit too confident, considering I had yet to learn how to swim on top of the water and still had to wear floaties when I went in the deep end.

One particular day, there was a large gathering of children and adults at my neighbor's pool. It must have been the Fourth of July, as it's hard to recall since I was only five or six at the time, and to be honest the next part of my story is the only part I remember vividly. It replays in my mind in slow motion as if I'm watching a movie. I must not have noticed while playing in the shallow end of the pool that I was near the area where it drops down to the deep end. I stepped back and before I knew it I was sliding down, and the water was suddenly over my head. I panicked. I couldn't move! I sank straight down and hit the bottom. If only I hadn't panicked I could have picked up my feet and done my mermaid swim over to the shallow side of the pool since it was only a few feet away.

I was so afraid, and all I could do was push really hard to get back up to the top, and I did, but I only managed to get just barely above the water. No one was looking. They didn't see me, and more panic set in immediately. I took a deep breath and sank back down to the bottom, and when my toes touched I pushed really hard again to get myself back up to the top, thinking someone would see me this time. Except I didn't go up as high, and still no one saw me. I remember thinking, *I'm going to drown* as I was sinking under the water. Exhausted and in slow motion, suddenly I was yanked up out of the water. It was my brother.

He saw me, the only one who saw me. He jumped in without a second thought or word to anyone else and pulled me up as fast as he could to save me from drowning. My thirteen-year-old brother saved my life. I was his aggravating bratty little sister, the baby, Mom's favorite. Or at least that's what I used to tell him. I was the little sister who told Mom everything he did wrong and laughed when he got into trouble. Typical brother and sister stuff.

My big brother in that moment forgot about everything I had ever done to him, and without a second thought he came through for me and showed his love to his annoying little sister. He loved me so much that he had been looking after me without me even knowing. I was so little at the time of the incident, and as an adult I am overwhelmed with gratitude for being alive. I don't think I have ever really expressed my gratitude to my brother for saving my life, until now."

Sirina carried around the events of that day with her for over thirty-five years, yet she can still feel the terror within her as if it happened yesterday. As she revisits that place in her subconscious mind, the feeling of terror is stirred up once again because the subconscious mind doesn't know the difference between what is real, fake, current, or in the past. That trauma has been lodged within her body for years, and she experiences an ongoing loop of distress every time that particular cellular memory is triggered.

I noticed tears in her eyes as she explained the thought of her possible drowning, and although it is still very real to her today, the tears she shed were from the realization that for years she allowed that thought to take over her life. The mind constantly wanders, and that's where her mind repeatedly took her. It wasn't until she openly shared her story and learned to replace the thought of almost dying with celebrating her life today that she was able to release the fear and embrace gratitude. Her whole being is now encompassed with heartfelt gratitude, and she shares that gratitude for her brother today.

Gratitude Is a State of Being

When you live in gratitude, it ensures peace, joy, and happiness. Life is way too precious to take anyone or anything for granted. Let this serve as a reminder for us all to take a deeper look within and extend gratitude to the ones we love and for all the many blessings in our lives. Being grateful in times of suffering doesn't mean you approve of or agree with your circumstances at hand, but it does mean that you are willing and able to look past those challenging times. That's because gratitude is a state of being. When you choose to be grateful no matter what, the energy of gratitude transcends whatever is going on around you and also enhances your vibration.

Developing a lasting habit to express gratitude for your future memories supports your dreams. Creating a life that you love commands gratitude if you want to see it manifest. Avoiding ingratitude and adopting an attitude of gratitude for your life will open the path to plenty. We sometimes think that being grateful is what we offer at the end after we have received the desires of our heart, but in truth by extending gratitude first those desires are made manifest. Intentionally savor the moments that the universe has shared with you.

Loving Reminders

- ♥ Gratitude is an essential virtue to live by.
- ♥ Gratitude is prayer in the highest form.
- ♥ Being grateful all the days of our lives is praying without ceasing.
- ♥ Cultivate an attitude of gratitude.
- ♥ Expressing gratitude is good for the heart.
- ♥ Gratitude is a mindset.
- ♥ Being grateful is a choice.
- ♥ Make a commitment to express daily gratitude.
- ♥ When you live in gratitude, it ensures peace, joy, and happiness.

TEN

CHOOSE LOVE

Gratitude creates a soothing underlying unity of absolute perfection. May you recognize even the smallest of pleasures it has to offer. There are countless ways to show gratitude, and the giving and receiving of benefits is endless. As we learn to recognize gratitude as a universal expression of love, it will foster expanded states of awareness. Gratitude needs no filter and is abundant in many forms.

As you become aware of and present to the love that you are, allow your radiance to illuminate the path for others. Be the one who consciously chooses love. Love for the inspiring possibility of life. Love over hate, love over judgment, love over jealousy, love over ridicule, and love over anything you can think of. Can you see yourself approaching everything with love? Just think about that for a minute. Think about how it could change the course of your day, weeks, months, years, and eventually the course of your life if you shifted your perception and approached everything with love. Not only is love one of the greatest gifts we could ever give to one another, but it will also raise your vibration and consciousness to a whole new level.

Simply Let Go

I think most of us have a general idea about forgiveness, gratitude, and love, but this time it was different for me. It felt deeper, and it undeniably had more meaning. My gradual awakening led me to discover that holding onto the old way of being was of no value to me any longer. Once I surrendered into the shift I stopped fighting myself. I simply let go of doubt, worry, and fear and put all my trust in God/Source/Universe/Spirit. It's as if I jumped into the ocean and allowed the waves to gently carry me. I stopped swimming upstream, constantly fighting the massive current.

By willingly releasing my anxious thoughts and tuning out the noises of the outside world, a blanket of calmness now covers me as I move forward in my spiritual journey. Feeling centered and at peace, I've enjoyed many beautiful revelations, and I gained a whole new perspective on life. Everything in my life started to shift as I engaged with the spiritual essence within. I felt like I was thrust into a truth-seeking adventure, and along the way I began to see the world around me so differently.

Respect the Path

I am humbled by the vastness of love in the universe. Love has been the absolute jewel of my journey in reconnecting to self. I had no idea of the wondrous experiences in store for me, like awakening to my truth, stepping into my power, and creating a life that I love.

Each of these were made possible because I chose to love myself through it, which allowed the pain and vulnerability to subside. Choosing to see the good in others and ourselves allows for healing from the inside out. We are all connected and interconnected through love, thus love will ultimately reveal itself as a graceful expression within every individual, either knowingly or unknowingly. We are eternally loving beings. Love is ever-present and equally measured throughout all life.

The one and only true path to life is love. We either make choices out of fear or out of love, and fear is just inverted faith. We certainly cannot deny how wonderful it feels when we are loved, and everyone wants to be loved and accepted by others. It wasn't until I learned to love myself unconditionally that I truly began to believe and understand that I am both worthy and whole. I learned to respect the path that has brought me to where I am today. No matter where I've been and no matter where I'm going in life, I vow not to give others the power to determine my self-worth. Never trade your authenticity for the approval of others.

We endure suffering when we don't nourish the soul with the love and goodness that we are. If we don't act on this and begin to see the good within ourselves, we will never be able to see the good within others. Hold a vision of love for yourself and demonstrate what love and self-love is. Just bathe in the pure essence of the love that you are. It is our true divine nature to be loving and kind. Be it, feel it, see it, and share it with the world. Your light, love, and spiritual essence are all contagious.

A Moment of Divine Connectedness

As you foster meaningful relationships in the interest of a marriage, a partnership, or even a friendship, remember to choose love as the foundation. Life is an echo. If you want more love, give more love. In fact, make it a part of your everyday living. Every interaction we are blessed to have with each other is an opportunity to grow. Allow your words to be seasoned with love and kindness. When we aspire to love ourselves first, we create an opening to love others wholly.

Recently, while vacationing with my husband, we were walking along a deserted beach holding hands and taking in the sound of the waves breaking against the shoreline. I don't think either one of us has ever heard such a profound sound. The waves roared like thunder as they crashed and rolled in. We were simply amazed. We found the perfect place to sit, and we dug our feet into the sand. We inhaled deeply, exhaled slowly, and listened intently. After staring at what seemed to be an endless ocean, our eyes automatically looked upward at the evening sky, as we were both in awe and captured by the beauty of our surroundings. I leaned in and laid my head on his chest as I wrapped my arm around the front of his waist, feeling a sense of peace even though the waves continued to pound the shore. The sound was almost hypnotic. He wrapped his arms around me and moments later whispered, "God sure did a great job."

Instantly the corners of my mouth lifted, and my eyes welled up with tears. My heart was overflowing with love and gratitude to be with this amazing man in that very moment. I just squeezed him as tightly as I could. I remember thinking that I wanted to remember that moment of boundless love moving to us and through us. What a delightful experience. It was magical sensing his love and gratitude for simply being alive and connecting with God that way, recognizing the miracles—including ourselves—that surrounded us. We were one with each other, with the sand, with the ocean, with the sky, and with the universe. We were fully present in divine connectedness. Having experienced that moment with my husband, I have gained a greater inspiration for what is to come. In the words of Emerson, "Love asks nothing but does all receive."

That moment marked a very important time in our lives. We were both in alignment with the recent choices we made for ourselves. Creating a life that we love by living intentionally and experiencing a deeper meaning to life through loving virtues agreed with us. We were both savoring the moment of that realization with the significance that it was the beginning of living from a place of knowing. I feel fortunate to have purposefully opened myself up, gone deep within, and questioned everything in my life. It has been a long process of healing through love—love of myself, and love for others. I cried a river of tears through awareness, celebration, pain, and understanding—and sometimes all in one day.

The Judgment-Free Challenge

In between the experiences of my shift, I thought I was the most loving person in the world. But a lot of healing had to take place for those words to become an expression of truth. I have since acknowledged that my reaction toward others was simply a way of protecting myself and hiding behind my own pain and insecurities. We all have the power within to build a better relationship with love, and once you begin to honor your feelings, you initiate the healing process. By doing so you are offering yourself loving guidance as opposed to deepening your pain of separation. By choosing love over judgment you become consciously aware of and present to the love that you are.

By setting the intention to cultivate love into everything I did, I had to become consciously aware of my thoughts and actions. So I asked myself this riveting question, and you may ask yourself the same: *Is what I am doing, thinking, or saying being done with love?* Beautiful souls, *how* you show up in the world truly counts. Change starts with the one in the mirror, and when you invite a positive transformation you become a change agent for the world. So if you answered no to that question then you already know that you have some internal work to do. Most of us do, and once I analyzed love from my newfound perspective and understanding, that's where I humbly found myself too.

Two amazing girlfriends and I decided to challenge both ourselves and our judgments. While the vast majority of people consider themselves to be unprejudiced, there are many who cast judgmental thoughts of criticism every single day. Realizing just how frequently judgment might arise, we have made it the habitual standard of conversation. You name it and people are judging it.

My judgment-free challenge revealed a part of myself that I didn't know existed, or at least I didn't realize it existed to the extent that it did. While paying attention to my inner dialogue, I realized just how often I had judgmental tendencies. I couldn't help but think there has to be a better way to live. Disturbingly enough, I've come to the conclusion that we are all basically beating each other up with our minds when we project negative thoughts toward one another. Choosing love over judgment is the obvious solution.

The challenge held me accountable for my actions and made me very aware of every thought, even toward myself. As quickly as a negative thought entered my mind, I immediately replaced it with a loving and positive thought. I was stunned when I actually paid attention to how quickly my mind chatter cast judgmental thoughts, and over the silliest of things too. This exercise has freed me to realize I don't have to congest my mind with distracting thoughts that are none of my business and don't even directly concern me. It was also empowering because it helped me gain better control over my own thought processes.

Remember, we are all responsible for our own thoughts and our thoughts create our environment. Let this serve as a reminder that you are misusing the power of your thoughts when you inflict judgment on another. Judgment creates division and only breeds more negativity.

The Veil of Assumptions

Self-judgment is a form of self-punishment. This can cause a great deal of mental and physical anguish. Judging others and ourselves is a tough pattern to break. Intuitively one may feel that it's wrong, but it usually doesn't stop there. Before they know it, the words of judgment are sliding off their tongue and leaping over their lips. One might have a sense of regret for their behavior, but often the human part of them wants to dance with the idea of judging others. The problem is that when we exercise judgment, we usually shrug it off as harmless thoughts flowing in and out of the mind. But at the core of every individual there are underlying issues going on.

When we judge, we are experiencing life through the veil of assumptions. It's easy to see the faults of others while we so casually overlook our own. Pay attention to how you feel right after you've expressed judgment, even for the smallest of things. Do you see something in others that you don't see in yourself? Be honest. Does it feel better to put someone else down rather than reflect on your own insecurities? Many will measure their self-worth according to what they see in others.

It's amazing to me how easily we can fall into the judgment trap. We judge our own appearances as well as others'. We judge someone who drives a beat-up old car, and we judge someone who drives a brand-new expensive car. We judge those who have addictions. We also judge those who are overweight and underweight. The list could go on and on. Unproductive thoughts such as these are constantly swirling in our minds attaching labels with the stamp of judgment to everything. When you judge others, it has *everything* to do with you and *nothing* to do with them. You are revealing a part of yourself that needs to be nurtured and healed.

The next time you express harsh judgment toward yourself or others, redirect your thinking and feelings toward love and compassion instead. Choose to remain in the energy of love. When we pass judgment, we are not in our hearts, we are in our egoic mind. It isn't until you remove the blinders of pride that you will be able to get to the core of who you really are. We prolong our growth by avoiding the real issues at hand. The next time you're with a group of people, pay attention to how the conversation unfolds. If it leads to gossip, be the one who's willing to shift the tone and direction. You'll be amazed at how wonderful you'll feel.

Many have spent a lifetime searching for love, wholeness, and happiness through the external things in their lives, but none of it will even matter if they don't choose to love themselves first. We have become our own worst enemy, using our minds against ourselves.

Although ego may have you think differently, no one is better than the next, just different. We are all unique, have different abilities, different professions, and live completely different lives, but we all have the same value. When you love yourself, you judge others less. When egos heal, love will effortlessly rise to the surface.

Wide Open

You can't control what others think or do, but you can certainly control your own behavior. In a world where there is judgment, hatred, conflict, fear, agony, and pain, be the light. Transform your life and the lives of those around you by choosing love. Give birth to a greater purpose and live your life wide open. All we have is today, so live your life to its fullest by making changes, not excuses.

Your outer world is a reflection of your inner thoughts. If you hold fear within, your world will reflect one of conflict, grudges, and struggle. If you hold love within, your world will reflect one of mercy, love, and forgiveness. You get to choose how you perceive your world within. What is your heart saying to you? What are you holding onto? Life is calling for you to expand in consciousness, and what will emerge is a more self-aware being.

As you shift into a higher version of yourself, you will experience a very personal transformation. Your life will resemble one of inner empowerment as you take on a more mindful approach to your everyday choices. Your transformation will only amplify your heart-centered alignment.

Gangsta to Goddess

I am so grateful to the courageous woman who embarked on a journey to transform her life. Little by little she broke through an invisible wall that separated her from the outside world. It isn't what she did in the progression of her growth that matters, it is who she became. Today that courageous woman is a more expansive being living a life that gives her life. There was a time when she felt like she lost herself inside of this great big old world, but once she stepped into her power, a beautiful illuminated path was formed.

There is meaning, fulfillment, acceptance, purpose, passion, and love present at all times, all of which she desired most in life. She learned that to experience the desires of her heart, she had to move through her current experiences of the reality she created for herself. By properly utilizing the universal laws and learning a new way to think, she overcame thoughts of adversity and created a life she loves, both on the inside and the outside. By maintaining faith with understanding, her life resembles one of harmony and ease. She lives with intention and chooses to exude forgiveness, gratitude, and love.

By shifting from an ego-based mentality into a higher version of myself through awareness, love, and understanding, the road to authenticity was paved. Little did I know that choosing to send love to myself at that seminar would be the key to unlocking my life. Shifting from Gangsta to Goddess seems so simple now, and today it casts a glowing reflection. Love. Love was the answer the whole time. Love is what fused all my little broken pieces together. Oh what a delightful downpour of bliss!

I have outgrown that tiny space where I used to live within the confines of my mind. It is truly a beautiful feeling when you can embrace yourself with self-love and admiration. Having a better understanding of who I am enables me to have a better understanding of others. I feel so alive and exuberant, and I know the possibilities that await. Profound changes lead to a profound life, and I am relishing every moment. When life presents itself as a challenge, I automatically return to love. That's the best part of my shift! What was not the norm has now become the norm, and I can't imagine living my life any other way.

Love Changes Everything

What it really boils down to is the betterment of ourselves. Transformation is the essence of spirituality. Trust in the power that is beckoning you to be, do, have, and give more. Be faithful to the most integral part of who you are. There is a beautiful life waiting to unfold for you. Nurture that part of you that wants to move forward. The entire world is waiting for your light. Don't be afraid to let it shine. In fact, let your light shine so brightly that others will be able to absorb it in excessive quantities. Remove the blinders of pride and begin to live your most loving, gracious, and authentic life. Let your love radiate, and one by one you will inspire others to do the same. Are you ready to dive deep within the capacity of love and self-love? Love is healing. Love is divine. Love changes everything. We must become more capable of love in all that we do. Choose love.

When you choose to see life through a lens of love, many of life's alluring experiences will draw you in, and something magical will happen. From this vantage point you begin to focus on the good of others, effortlessly being able to see past any mistakes. You will discover a beautiful space of all the infinite possibilities and a love so grand that it cannot be denied. The world around you will be full of brilliance as you infuse love in all that you do, all that you feel, all that you see, all that you say, and all that you are. Your perspective on life will change significantly, and the joy of being alive will be in full effect. It will seem as if a curtain has been lifted, revealing all the beautiful hidden expressions of life.

Loving Reminders:

- ♥ Be the one who consciously chooses love.
- ♥ Love is the greatest gift we could ever give to one another.
- ♥ We are eternally loving beings.
- ♥ The one and only true path to life is love.
- ♥ Never trade your authenticity for the approval of others.
- ♥ We endure suffering when we don't nourish the soul with the love and goodness that we are.
- ♥ By choosing love over judgment you become consciously aware of and present to the love that you are.
- ♥ How you show up in the world truly counts.
- ♥ Self-judgment is a form of self-punishment.
- ♥ Choose to remain in the energy of love.
- ♥ Profound changes lead to a profound life.
- ♥ What it really boils down to is the betterment of ourselves.
- ♥ Trust in the power that is beckoning you to be, do, have, and give more.
- ♥ We must become more capable of love in all that we do.